# The Origins and Development of the European Union 1945–95

before the last date shown below.

LEEDS COLLEGE OF BUILDING
WITHDRAWN FROM STOCK

LEEDS COLLEGE OF BUILDING

T16186

LEEDS COLLEGE OF BUILDING LIBRARY
CLASS NO. 337 142 T 16186
BARCODE

# The Origins and Development of the European Union 1945–95

A history of European integration

Martin J. Dedman

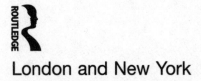

London and New York

First published 1996
by Routledge
11 New Fetter Lane, London EC4P 4EE

Simultaneously published in the USA and Canada
by Routledge
29 West 35th Street, New York, NY 10001

*Routledge is an International Thomson Publishing company*

© 1996 Martin J. Dedman

Typeset in Baskerville by Routledge
Printed and bound in Great Britain by Clays Ltd, St Ives PLC

All rights reserved. No part of this book may be reprinted or
reproduced or utilised in any form or by any electronic, mechanical,
or other means, now known or hereafter invented, including
photocopying and recording, or in any information storage or
retrieval system, without permission in writing from the publishers.

*British Library Cataloguing in Publication Data*
A catalogue record for this book is available from the British Library

*Library of Congress Cataloguing in Publication Data*
A catalogue record for this book has been requested

ISBN 0–415–11161–7

*To my mother, Peggy Dedman, and my late father, W.G. Dedman*

# Contents

# Acknowledgements

I am grateful to colleagues Dr Duncan Ross, Mike Denton and Clive Fleay at Middlesex University and also to Frank Swartz of the Institute of Historical Research for their helpful comments on early drafts of this book; to Ruby Norris for her dedication and thoroughness in word-processing most of this text; and finally to my wife, Dr Catherine Sandler, for all her encouragement and help over the past year.

Acknowledgement is made to the Fondation Jean Monnet pour l'Europe, Lausanne, for permission to reproduce the cover photograph showing Jean Monnet in the Silesian coalfields.

# Abbreviations

| | |
|---|---|
| BTO | Brussels Treaty Organization |
| CAP | Common Agricultural Policy |
| CDU | Christlich Demokratische Union |
| CEEC | Committee of European Economic Co-operation |
| CET | Common External Tariff |
| CFEU | Conseil Français pour l'Europe Uni |
| CUSG | Customs Union Study Group |
| DGB | German Federation of Trades Unions |
| Dom-Toms | Departments and Territories of Metropolitan France |
| EC | European Community |
| ECSC | European Coal and Steel Community |
| EDC | European Defence Community |
| EEA | European Economic Area |
| EEC | European Economic Community |
| EFTA | European Free Trade Association |
| EIB | European Investment Bank |
| EMS | European Monetary System |
| EMU | European Monetary Union |
| EP | European Parliament |
| EPC | European Political Community |
| EPU | European Payments Union |
| ERDF | European Regional Development Fund |
| ERM | Exchange Rate Mechanism |
| ERP | European Recovery Programme |
| ESF | European Social Fund |
| EU | European Union |
| FRG | Federal Republic of Germany (West Germany) |
| FTA | Free Trade Area |
| FURI | Federal Union Research Institute |

| | |
|---|---|
| GATT | General Agreement on Tariffs and Trade |
| GDP | Gross Domestic Product |
| GDR | German Democratic Republic (East Germany) |
| GNP | Gross National Product |
| NATO | North Atlantic Treaty Organization |
| NCB | National Coal Board |
| NIC | Newly Industrialized Country |
| NTB | Non Tariff Barrier |
| OECD | Organization for Economic Co-operation and Development |
| OEEC | Organization for European Economic Co-operation |
| OPEC | Organization of Petroleum Exporting Countries |
| PEU | Pan European Union |
| PRO | Public Record Office |
| QMV | Qualified Majority Voting |
| RPF | Rassemblement du Peuple Français |
| SEA | Single European Act |
| SFIO | Section Française de l'Internationale Ouvrière (French Socialist Party) |
| SPD | Sozialdemocratische Partie Deutschlands |
| TUC | Trades Union Congress |
| UEF | Union Européene des Fédéralistes |
| UEM | United Europe Movement |
| VAT | Value Added Tax |
| WEU | Western European Union |

# Prologue

The title of this book might seem a misnomer as the Treaty on European Union (EU) was only signed in February 1992 (following agreement at the Maastricht summit by member states' heads of government in December 1991). The EU's ratification process was only completed in 1993. Yet in reality the EU is currently mainly a continuation of the European Economic Community (EEC) 1958–86, and the European Community (EC) 1986–91, under a different name or guise. Despite the EU Treaty incorporating the objective of Economic and Monetary Union by 1999, the extent of any constitutional change to date is modest. It has amounted to cosmetic surgery rather than to a metamorphosis of the institutions and functions of the EC (see Chapter 6).

The EU's fifteen member states and its 'single market' of 360 million people now account for more than 40 per cent of world trade (cf. 9 per cent for Japan) and the queue of Mediterranean, Central and Eastern European countries wanting to join stretches into the future. The fact that, after 45 years of existence, the EU's integrated organisation appeals to so many independent nation states is testimony to its attractiveness and success.

How did all this start? Why did only six states initially involve themselves in economic integration? What ideas and influences shaped the organisation? Was federation the motive?

This book aims to answer such questions and to strip away the rhetoric surrounding European integration that belies the often more mundane reality of fact. The story of the EEC is a subject that is often quite mistakenly wrapped in all sorts of assumptions regarding its supposed purpose and goal.

Certainly the institutional framework of the 1951 European Coal and Steel Community (ECSC), EEC and EU were part of a continual resolution of Western Europe's fundamental predicament. Since the

end of World War II in 1945 Western Europe has faced two big problems –
Germany and Russia. How to live safely and securely with them remains
the fundamental question facing Europe today. The reason for this is the
experience and record of the past. In the case of Germany there have been
conflicts in 1864, 1870, 1914–18 and most catastrophically 1939–45. For
France, which was invaded three times in 70 years, Germany was always
the bigger of the two problems. In 1940 France had to surrender in the
same railway carriage in which Germany had signed the Armistice in
1918. It had taken Hitler less than 6 weeks to humble a historic foe.
Germany's victory march through Paris in 1940 followed the identical
route to the French victory march of 1918. To end a recurring cycle of
vengeance and war was uppermost in French minds. De Gaulle's post-war
government in 1944 even signed the shortlived Treaty of Moscow with the
USSR, a mutual defence pact which named the potential aggressor as
Germany. Between 1944–48 French policy towards Germany was to try
and keep it weak and dismembered, on the principle that 'French strength
lay in German weakness'.

In 1948 France had to come to terms politically with the reality of an
emergent West German state and strong economy. These factors plus the
economic necessity of access to German markets and coal supplies
produced a volte-face in French policy. A Franco-German alliance has
subsequently been the bedrock and motor of European economic
integration. It flourished from the Adenauer–de Gaulle era, in 1958–
63, up to that of Kohl and Mitterrand in the 1980s.

The objective of safely incorporating a revived German economy into
Western Europe, in the absence of any formal peace settlement with the
defeated, belligerent former Germany, was solved through economic
integration: the creation of common markets originally in coal and steel in
1951 and in industrial goods in 1957. This meant that the recovery of
German economic power did not pose a political or military threat to
Europe in the 45 years following World War II. (Whereas Japan's rise to
economic superpower status has alarmed its Asian neighbours.)

The institutional creations (ECSC, EEC) of European economic
integration also formed part of the post-war 'architecture' of what was
called 'containment'. This was US President Harry Truman's policy at the
start of the 'Cold War' in 1947 of keeping the USSR behind its 1945
frontiers and stopping the further spread of Soviet communism. From
1947 the US sponsored and encouraged all forms of integration in
Europe. Europe was divided by the 'Iron Curtain' into two blocs each
within a superpower's sphere of influence – the USSR's in Eastern Europe
and the USA's in Western Europe.

Stalin's policy of 'defensive expansionism' turned East and Central European states liberated by the Red Army in World War II into communist states. This westward extension of the 'Soviet Empire' resulted in a chain of 'buffer states'; an insurance against possible future invasion from the west which also violated the wartime agreement made at Yalta in January 1945 when Stalin agreed with Roosevelt and Churchill to the principles of self-determination and free elections for liberated Europe. At the end of the war the two powers who had previously contained the USSR – Germany and Japan – were both defeated. The North Atlantic Treaty Organization (NATO), established in 1949 (a permanent peace-time military alliance operating on the principle of mutual defence – 'an attack on one being an attack on all'), and American atomic weapons, deterred the USSR militarily. However, security from Soviet communism and a resurgent Germany was not simply a military issue: it was also fundamentally economic. Economic growth and higher living standards in Western Europe from the late 1940s through to the 1980s enhanced its security against communist influence. Political stability, particularly democratic stability, depended on a sufficient level of comfort and economic satisfaction. European integration, through a common market, provided a superior framework for facilitating this than Comecon (the Council of Mutual Economic Assistance, established in 1949 as a Soviet reaction to Marshall Aid and the OEEC) and the centrally planned command economies of the Soviet Empire's Eastern Bloc.

The radical changes to the European map following the geopolitical upheavals of 1989–91 upset the balance of power in Europe that had existed since 1945, and marked the end of the post-war era and the old certainties of the Cold War. The fall of the Berlin Wall in November 1989, the peaceful collapse of communist regimes in Eastern Europe (with the exception of Romania), the end of the Warsaw Pact and Comecon and, ultimately, in December 1991 the demise of the USSR itself, were events of seismic proportions comparable to the French Revolution two hundred years before in 1789–91 or the Russian Revolution of 1917.

Before 1989–91 the big questions were what Russia's intentions were and what action might they take. Since 1991, with the end of any conventional military threat of invasion to Western Europe from the Red Army, these same questions also relate to the newly reunified Germany with a population of 80 million and with the world's fourth largest GDP. How will this affect the future shape of Europe? Will the European Union become a larger, more loosely organised and less-integrated community in which Germany might be free to decide its own foreign policy and, like Bismarck's Germany after 1870, become the 'pivot of Europe'? Germany could perhaps translate its economic power into political and military hegemony in Central and Eastern Europe; or will the European Union become a more 'integrated community' with Germany the leading power among 15 and soon more states with the German mark as its anchor?

All of these issues mean that the EU and its development has an important role and an enduring relevance for the future.

# Part I

## Origins

# Chapter 1

# Definition and theories of European integration, 1945–95

What are the distinguishing characteristics of an integrated organisation as opposed to other international organisations that governments join? Professor Alan Milward and Vibeke Sorensen made the distinction clear between integrated and interdependent organisations (Milward *et al.*, 1993, chapter 1). International organisations such as the Organization of Co-operation and Development (OECD), the General Agreement on Tariffs and Trade (GATT) and the North Atlantic Treaty Organization (NATO) operate on the basis of 'interdependence', i.e. a group of national governments co-operate together in certain policy areas, agreements are made based on mutual co-operation. Such organisations do not interfere with the policy-making of their member states, their decisions do not overrule national policies and there is little if any power or sanction to impose policies on member states. This is the most common type of international organisation or basis of agreement.

Integration, however, requires the creation of a 'supranational organisation' such as the European Coal and Steel Community (ECSC) 1951, and the European Economic Community (EEC) 1957. Here the member states transfer some policy decisions to a body of all member states, the decisions of which are binding on all members and have to be followed. So member states within supranational organisations transfer some power (sovereignty) to that organisation. Furthermore, the supranational organisation has the power to impose sanctions on member governments, in cases of non-compliance with policy decisions or breaches of agreements. For example, in the EEC one of the functions of the European Commission is to act as a 'policeman' to ensure compliance and another EEC organ, the European Court of Justice, makes legal judgements (that take precedence over member states' national law) in cases of dispute.

What are the practical benefits of integrated supranational organisations over international interdependent bodies? While acknowledging that the administrative and other costs are higher, Milward and Sorensen (1993) identify three key advantages of European economic integration. In the first place the agreements were 'irreversible' (or at least less easily reversed). The Rome Treaty 1957 establishing the EEC set no time limit, i.e. it is intended to be of an indefinite duration. This is unusual; treaties normally are for prescribed periods, which can be extended (the NATO Treaty 1949 was originally for 20 years) or have to be renegotiated (e.g. the original Non-Proliferation Treaty 1963, where states agreed not to acquire nuclear weapons, that expired in 1995). The Rome Treaty also contains no procedures for members to leave the European Economic Community (Greenland left the EEC but this was after achieving independence from Denmark). The significance of these points is that integration provides a much greater guarantee that agreements and policies once made will be adhered to continuously. Such arrangements are therefore secure as there is more certainty that deals struck between nation states will continue and not be broken. (The importance of this is underlined by the instance when Nazi Foreign Minister Joachim von Ribbentrop presented Adolf Hitler on his birthday with a casket containing copies of all the treaties he had broken!)

The second advantage of supranational organisations is their 'exclusiveness' as an integrated body. The six members of the EEC from 1957 onwards could exclude other prospective members unless they accepted their terms, the 'acquis communitaire' concept, i.e. new members have to agree to accept all the 'club' rules. This makes the integrated organisation a strong cohesive force, enhances its bargaining position with outsiders and provides it with the potential to discriminate. Britain in 1955 at first joined but then withdrew from the talks that established the EEC in 1957. Then in 1961 when Britain decided to join after all, it was excluded by de Gaulle (Britain joined 12 years later on its third attempt) and was discriminated against by the Common External Tariff – the EEC's protectionist tariff wall.

The third advantage of an integrated organisation according to Milward *et al.* is that they are more 'law abiding'. The Treaty of Paris 1951 and Treaties of Rome 1957 created a new legal system and framework to regulate both the institutions' and members' powers, rights and obligations.

The institutional arrangements for European economic integration in the 1950s were part of the solution to the big question facing Western Europe – how to live safely with Germany and the USSR.

However, whilst this helps explain the integrated organisational form adopted it does not specifically answer why it was that the ECSC 1951 and the EEC 1957 were set up. Why did six governments sign these two treaties? Why did other governments refuse to join? Why, too, does it appear that only economic integration succeeds? (Attempts at non-economic 'integration' have, like the European Defence Community (EDC) of 1950–54, collapsed.)

There are three schools of thought offering explanations for European integration. Most textbooks on the European Community contain a chapter on 'origins' that weaves a story based on the first two types of explanation examined here.

The orthodox explanation for European integration is not historical at all but drawn from political science. The argument is that the increased complexity of both the post-1945 international order and the range and functions of the modern nation state mean that countries are inexorably entwined in a network of functioning international bodies (such as NATO, the United Nations (UN), or GATT), and the scope for independent action by individual states is curtailed by collective decision taking. It is further argued that once integrated organisations are established there is an inevitable tendency for further integration to occur so that the ECSC 1951 led to the EEC 1957 or the Single European Act (SEA) 1986 led to the objective of Economic and Monetary Union (EMU) in the EU Treaty 1992. So, once European integration has started it becomes a self-sustaining process, powered by Brussels Eurocrats, resulting in the piecemeal incremental integration of Europe. This process is expected to result in a Federal United States of Europe. The inevitable result of increasing the scope of an integrated supranational organisation is the eventual demise of the nation state whose functions, responsibilities and sovereignty are transferred to the supranational state (George, 1992; Haas, 1958; Milward *et al.*, 1993).

As we shall see, this orthodox explanation appears less than satisfactory as an interpretation of the facts, namely the limited extent of integration over the past 40 years. The fact is that it has been exclusively economic and that decision-making (and so political power) still lies with national governments acting together within the European Union. The European Commission makes proposals, it does not take decisions. The European Parliament is not a legislature, it has always had the right to be consulted and now has some 'codecision' rights, but has never passed a law. in 40 years. Political power in the European Community lies with the member states: decisions are taken collectively by them within the Council of Ministers. It seems highly improbable that the integration process inevitably leads to the disappearance of the nation state and the creation of a federal Europe. Whereas in the 1960s this undoubtedly appeared a plausible outcome and was enshrined in this orthodox explanation, its validity as a theory now looks unconvincing in the light of recent historical analysis of governments' archival records from the 1950s.

The second school of thought attributes European integration to the ideas, growth and influence of European federalist movements particularly from World War II (1939–45) onwards. Professor Walter Lipgens, the main exponent of this view, undertook detailed studies of the numerous movements and organisations advocating European federalism, the nurturing and development of the ideas in various wartime non-communist resistance movements in occupied Europe as well as the intrigue and ideological disputes between the various post-war pressure groups. Lipgens regards Euro-federalism as an inevitable and logical post-war policy based on the ideas and proposals of the resistance movements and the UK's 'Federal Union' 1939–41. Furthermore, he claims that lobbying and publicity by European federalist movements after 1945 resulted in moves to implement Euro-federal ideas, the outcome being the first supranational authority in 1950.

Lipgens' thesis is that a combination of the inherent logic of a federal solution for Europe (as an antidote to the destructive forces of total war, the Holocaust's genocide, totalitarianism, extreme nationalism and human rights abuses of the period 1933–45), the public support and promotion of federalism from politicians and intelligentsia, and a rising groundswell of mass public support for the idea failed to achieve complete fruition only because of two impediments. What Lipgens referred to as the 'first obstacle' was the declared antipathy of both the US and USSR between 1943–47 towards the idea of a federal Europe. However with the beginning of Soviet–American superpower rivalry in the Cold War from 1947–48, the US became an interested convert and then an enthusiastic advocate of Euro-federal solutions. However, by then a 'second opposing force' was West European governments themselves (who would have had to approve and implement any federation). For Lipgens the British, Scandinavian and French governments were 'bastions of stubborn nationalist traditions' and therefore the federal idea never achieved a real breakthrough.

Nevertheless, Lipgens argues that between 1945–55 when 'the policies for European Union were taking shape the political pressure groups advocating Union or federation were especially important; one cannot understand or describe the pre-history of the European movement or its beginnings without studying the activity of these groups'. The Union

Européenne de Fédéralistes (UEF) emerged from the Hertenstein meeting in December 1946 (its membership doubling to 200,000 between 1947–50). According to Lipgens' the UEF by 'increasingly successful lobbying made a big contribution to the integration effort between 1950–54'. However the only instance of successful lobbying by the UEF cited by Lipgens was Article 38 of the European Defence Community Treaty which assigned to its future parliament the task of framing a European constitution (Lipgens, 1982, pp. 12, 85; 1980, p. 119). The EDC/EPC attempt at integration collapsed – rejected by the French national assembly in August 1954. The only example Lipgens provides for successful influence and lobbying by European federalist movements was for an aborted scheme. Lipgens asserts that the European federalist movements influenced the earlier ECSC 1951 but no supportive evidence is provided. However he admits that after the miscarriage of the EDC scheme the European federalist movements had little or no influence over the subsequent Rome Treaties of 1957 (Lipgens, 1980, p. 137), which remain the principal instances of European economic integration establishing a common market in the European Economic Community and a joint programme for developing atomic energy in Euratom. Also, as Professor Alan Milward shows, Jean Monnet, 'the father of European integration', appears completely uninterested and uninvolved with European federalist movements between 1945–48 and is never mentioned by Lipgens in his studies. Furthermore, Monnet's conversion to the idea of European integration was apparently due initially to American – not European federalist – influence (Milward, 1992, p. 335). It was Jean Monnet who was responsible for starting the scheme for the ECSC.

Lipgens' thesis that the European integration of the 1950s was somehow the inevitable outcome of the European federalist movements' pressure and influence is hard to sustain, given the absence of real linkage between the transnational political pressure groups working for a European federation and the actual integrated organisations established by governments in the 1950s. Nevertheless, the European federalist movements remain more than an interesting intellectual and political phenomenon, as the following chapter will show, resulting in the tangible institutional development of the Council of Europe.

Lipgens' focus on the history of European federalist movements as an explanation for what followed appears superficially attractive and plausible but it inevitably ignores all the evidence drawn from national governments' archives that reveal the internal departmental debates over policy options and objectives involved and the basis for decisions taken.

Such documentary evidence, as subsequent chapters show, reveals that the motives and intentions of the six states that signed the Treaty of Paris 1951 and Treaties of Rome 1957 did not (rhetoric aside) include 'federation'.

Nevertheless, it might reasonably be contended that even if the European federalist movements' direct influence over the practice and procedures of European integrated bodies was minimal at least their long publicised prescriptions and prognoses for Europe were relevant. This may be so but their advocacy of a Customs Union (the central mechanism in both the ECSC and EEC) was an old idea: the *Zollverein* centred on Prussia was a Customs Union, incorporating many of the German states as early as 1833, and 1931–32 saw two proposals for Customs Unions between Germany and Austria, and by Belgium and Luxembourg in the Ouchy Convention July 1932.

The third type of explanation of European integration is entirely historical, based on the work of political, diplomatic and economic historians. The '30-year rule' meant that from the early 1980s British government documents covering the establishment of the ECSC and EEC three decades before became available. Through the use of Foreign Office, Board of Trade and Cabinet papers in the Public Record Office, the British government's rather dismal record of decision-making on Europe has been written up by historians such as John Young, Saki Dockrill and others, while economic historians such as Alan Milward and Frances Lynch have tapped into government and economic records in the UK and other European States involved in the integration process.

Alan Milward has produced a thesis firmly based and derived from empirical evidence (drawn from different national archives) to explain the origins and motivations for European integration. In essence the 'Milward thesis' states that European integration only occurs and only works when it is actually needed by nation states, there being no fundamental antagonism between European integration (seen in the ECSC and EEC) and the nation state. This stands in marked contrast to the other two types of explanation, both of which rest on the idea that European integration ultimately results in the demise of the nation state and the creation of a new supranational state or Federal United States of Europe. Milward says that supranational organisations were set up by the nation states for their own specific purposes, not as a step towards the submission and eclipse of the nation state within a federal Europe. The fundamental issue is: where does power lie? Whether in the EEC of the 1960s or European Union of 1990s, power remains with the nation states: all decisions are taken by the member states' governments collectively in the Council of Ministers (either by unanimity or qualified majority voting depending on the issue). The actual extent of surrender, or pooling of national control, to supranational organisations in Brussels decades later are still quite modest and restricted to some, but not all forms of economic activity. The supranational organisation has changed its name from EEC (1958–86) to European Community (1986–91) to European Union since Maastricht, yet it has remained a common or single market primarily concerned with common commercial issues and their related policies. There is, for example, still no such thing as a single common foreign policy for all EU members (although co-ordinated responses are attempted on specific issues). The only policy elements that members have integrated relate to economic or commercial affairs.

Milward argues further that European integration, far from advancing the cause of federation, actually 'rescued the nation state' – the supranational organisations ECSC and EEC were originally created by six states (France, Benelux, Italy and West Germany) because of economic necessity and political security. Euro-federalist ideas and movements, according to Milward's thesis, had nothing at all to do with European integration. He argues that the requirements of economic reconstruction and national rebuilding in Western Europe following World War II, from 1945 onwards, often required international solutions. This was because national governments were not able successfully to pursue their own plans for economic reconstruction in isolation from their neighbours, as they needed access to their West European neighbours' markets and raw materials (e.g. German coking coal). At the same time, in the late 1940s and early 1950s there was no free trade in Western Europe. Tariffs and quota restrictions to protect national markets were the norm.

West European states were mutually dependent economically yet rigged their own markets for national advantage. Also, national reconstruction plans were very similar in aim (increasing steel production figured prominently in French and others' schemes for national economic regeneration from 1946). This accounts for the necessity of commercial agreement between states. The Treaty of Paris 1951 established the ECSC, a common market in coal and steel, which resolved these problems and facilitated the attainment of national economic objectives in an international context.

Milward argues that when national reconstruction plans depended on economic links with West Germany, then integration occurred. An integrated rather than an interdependent organisation was created because of its intrinsic advantages. Milward shows that West German economic revival was crucial in the European economic system – it was the main source of machines and machine tools for its continental neighbours and a big consumer of food and steel. Dutch, French, Belgium and other states all needed to restore secure trading connections with West Germany. Their economic recovery and national reconstruction hinged to a large extent on German economic revival (Milward, 1992, pp. 155–67; 1984, pp. 492–502).

West Germany's political future in Europe was also of central importance. According to Milward, European economic integration took place when rebuilding nation states' economies after 1945 depended on economic links and agreement with Germany and so intersected with the 'big question', i.e. how to fix Germany safely and securely in Western Europe. Then and only then did European integration occur because it was a much more secure, permanent, law-abiding arrangement.

Paradoxically, according to Milward's thesis, far from European integration being a move towards creating a federal union in Western Europe, it was the mechanism by which a Federal Republic of Germany (West Germany) could safely re-emerge as another nation state. The process of European integration was not a first step to subsume Germany or other states in a federation but actually provided the means by which a new German state could be re-established and co-exist, in the absence of any treaty or formal peace settlement, with those western neighbours it had invaded, defeated and occupied 10–15 years before. West Germany was only freed from external post-war controls over its steel and coal production (ending the international Ruhr Authority's restrictions over coal exports from West Germany) within the confines of the ECSC from 1951. Similarly, within the context of the European Defence Community plan of 1950–54 (the failed integrated scheme to solve the vexed issue of German rearmament) under its Bonn Agreements full sovereignty was restored in foreign affairs and national defence from 1955 to the West German State.

Lipgens attributes European integration to the influence and lobbying of the European federalist movements before 1955 and for some political scientists integration once started is seen as an irreversible and inevitable process of transferring power and sovereignty from the nation state to a supranational state. The Milward thesis regards European integration as a creation of nation states for their own national purposes – the most secure means to achieve national economic policy objectives was by integration. For Milward both the Treaty of Paris 1951 (establishing the ECSC) and the Treaties of Rome 1957 (creating the EEC/Euratom) were primarily commercial treaties – the supranational components were there chiefly because of the German question.

The value of these three schools of thought as interpretations of the driving forces behind integration can be assessed in the following chapters, which trace the development of schemes for European integration between 1945 and 1995.

# Chapter 2

# The impact and significance of the European federalist movements and the Council of Europe (1949)

Movements to unite Europe politically only emerged post-World War I (although the idea originated as far back as the seventeenth century). The horror and carnage of World War I (1914–18) was the motivation behind this wish to end the destructive antagonistic rivalry of European nation states. Count Richard Coudenhove-Kalergi established the Pan-European Union in 1923 as a non-party mass movement for the unification of Europe; another organisation, the Association for European Co-operation, was started in Geneva in 1926 and had committees in Paris, Berlin and London. The interwar years also saw the early advocacy of a European Customs Union and a recommendation for a single market from 1920 in the face of increasing Japanese and US exports, economic stagnation, economic nationalism and tariff protectionism in Europe. In September 1929 Aristide Briand proposed the creation of a European Federal Union at the Assembly of the League of Nations which was viewed with incomprehension by most other ministers and statesmen, though interestingly not by Winston Churchill, who published articles supporting the idea of a 'United States of Europe' in 1930 and 1938. Churchill believed, however, that Britain was not part of Europe but should support it from outside and that the French and Germans should create it.

However, interest in such movements and proposals had no effect on the realities of European economic and political affairs and such organisations never achieved a mass following but remained a minority preoccupation of certain intellectuals (Lipgens, 1982, pp. 35–42; 1985, pp. 5–7).

The Bolsheviks in Russia were dismissive and contemptuous of federalist schemes for Europe and the Nazis after 1933 banned all pro-European associations as pacifist.

Lipgens argues that the experience of World War II had an overwhelming formative influence on the prospects and nature of European federalist ideas. It changed everything. It increased support for federal ideas as Europe's status diminished compared with that of the super-powers: the US and USSR. Experience of conquest and occupation under Nazi rule and the failure of national governments to provide the minimum of security and independence supposedly weakened public confidence in the nation state and strengthened federalist support.

Lipgens suggests, rather surprisingly, that wartime occupation in Nazi Europe accustomed people to a continental-style unified economy. A single centrally controlled economy under the Nazis was in fact more influential than ten years' work of the Pan-European Union as it showed the possibilities for a peacetime single European economy (Lipgens, 1985, pp. 8–9).

A federal state with supranational powers was invariably advocated by non-communist wartime Resistance movements (i.e. a majority of the Resistance) whether French, Dutch or Polish. According to Lipgens, the Resistance hardly ever favoured a return to the pre-war system of nation states in their leaflets and programmes. For example Philippe Viannay on 'The Future of Germany' in *Défense de la France* (no. 12 (Paris) 20 March 1942), spoke of Germany being integrated into a 'truly European order' and Claude Bourdet (leader of the non-communist Resistance) in *Combat, Organe de Mouvement de Libération National* (no. 55 (Lyons), March 1944), distinguished between the Nazi system and the German people and recognised that the Versailles Treaty was in part to blame for the Nazis' rise to power. He urged that at the end of the war, after the guilty had been punished, Germans should have equal rights with other European nations and Germany join a European federation on equal footing.

Altiero Spinelli, interned on the island of Ventotene by Mussolini in World War II, founded the Movimento Federalista Europeo inside the Italian Resistance and wrote the 'Ventotene Manifesto'. In *The United States of Europe*, he advocated a federal Europe to overcome 'international anarchy'. He argued that this was the true cause of racism and two world wars, for which neither democracies nor communists had the answer, only federalism.

Resistance publications towards the end of the war emphasised that they did not want a new 'Holy Alliance' of 'three great powers' over Europe but wanted instead a supranational European federation with political, military and judicial institutions to maintain peace, freedom and national independence. Liberty and civilisation would only be assured, after the barbarity of World War II, if a Federal Union replaced the existing anarchy of 30 European states (Lipgens, 1985, pp. 674–5; 1986, pp. 213, 214).

The somewhat grandiose sounding International Conference of Resistance Fighters held a clandestine meeting in May 1944 in Geneva (attended by 15 individuals, some of whom were refugees, representing nine nationalities). In their declarations they outlined most comprehensively the arguments for European federalism. Only a European federation would enable the German people to join European life without being a danger to other peoples; it would avoid any recurrence of aggression while recognising that Europe needed the German economy.

A European federation would ensure peace, avoid extreme nationalism, stop 'European civil wars' and allow the exercise of common powers over foreign political security matters and economic planning on a European scale.

A common market was considered by the 1944 Conference to be an economic necessity to avoid the problems associated with the economic crisis of the 1930s, while recognising the interdependence of European national economies. Article V also referred to the integration of 'German chemical and heavy industries into the European industrial organisation so as to prevent their use for German nationalistic ends'. The Conference recognised that Europe could only reassert itself between the two superpowers of the US and USSR if it federated (Lipgens, 1982, pp. 53–5; 1985, pp. 678–82).

Why exactly did European resistance movements come to advocate federalist solutions? Was it perhaps partly because the alternative solution to safe co-existence with a revived Germany was dismemberment of the German state? This was unacceptable to European federalists (though not to the French government of 1945–48), especially as there were two German representatives at the 1944 Conference. There was also a general recognition of the central role of the German economy within Europe's economy. Second, the pre-1939 League of Nations model to prevent war had completely failed and needed replacing in Europe. Third, federalist objectives were adopted as part of post-war planning to help sustain popular revolt *against* Nazi rule and *for* something to replace it.

How far did such federalist ideas penetrate? How influential were they? Lipgens admits that the ideas of the Resistance did not penetrate too far into the mass of the population. Even in the Resistance, federalism was far from being a homogeneous view. Many in the Maquis saw their fight as a purely national struggle (Lipgens, 1982, p. 60; 1985, p. 24). The highest circulation of any Resistance journal was 450,000 for *Défense de la France*, no. 43, January 1944.

Do these ideas, plans and programmes have any significance or are they simply part of the ephemera of intellectual history? The arguments of the Resistance leadership for federalism differed from the interwar period (which was reacting against the slaughter of 1914–18) and stressed a geo-political and economic rationale. The Resistance emphasised the need to regulate the 'nation state system' within a federal framework and so curb national sovereignty through a strong supranational authority to avoid the brutality of totalitarianism and preserve human rights.

There is a continuity in aim and rationale between the Resistance, the post-war European federalist movements and some organisations and institutions that were created between 1947 and 1957. This does not mean that there was a causal connection but merely that the wartime Resistance's agenda for post-war Europe had an enduring logic and relevance.

Britain's experience of the approach and outbreak of war between the Munich Agreement 1938 and the fall of France in June 1940 triggered a brief surge of interest in European federalism in Britain. John Pinder's research revealed 'the remarkable body of literature on plans for federation published between 1939–41 ... it is doubtful, despite the flow of material in the post war years, whether such an impressive amount has appeared in any one country since'. W.B. Curry's *The Case for Federal Union*, a Penguin Special, Autumn 1939, sold 100,000 copies in six months. This text and others developed the theme that the basic cause of war was national sovereignty and that it could be prevented through common federal government managing common affairs. The same argument appeared later in Resistance literature.

Pinder makes the point that the 'literature attained a coherence and force' because it appeared within the framework of two organisations set up in 1939–40: the 'Federal Union' and in 1940 the Federal Union Research Institute (FURI). Federal Union's membership was growing at a rate of 500 a month by December 1939 and between 1939–40 it recruited 10,000 people in 200 branches (Pinder, 1986, pp. 26–8). Although started by three unknown people, it soon attracted distinguished support from, for example, Barbara Wootton, the Labour politician; Lord Lothian, an ex-Liberal minister and Washington Ambassador; and Wickham Steed, ex-Editor of the *Times*. Federal Union organised big meetings, printed a weekly news sheet and its first conference in March 1940 appointed to its council prominent academics and politicians including William Bever-idge, C.E.M. Joad and Ivor Jennings, the constitutional lawyer. The Federal Union Research Institute started work in the summer of 1939 and was formally established in March 1940 to investigate the technicalities of federation under the chairmanship of Beveridge, then Master of University College Oxford. A brilliant group of experts produced studies on constitutional, economic and other aspects of federation within FURI. Indeed, the Economics Committee anticipated many of the issues that have subsequently arisen in the EEC (a common currency, complete free trade, fixed exchange rates, free labour migration). Ivor Jennings' *A Federation of Western Europe*, 1940, was the first FURI publication and drew up a Federal Constitution. Lionel Robbins' *Economic Causes of War*, 1939, made a powerful case for a European federation, as did Sir W. Beveridge's *Peace by Federation?*, Federal Tracts, no. 1 (Federal Union), 1940.

British federalist literature 1939–41 had an enormous influence on continental federalists, particularly in Italy. Alterio Spinelli obtained Federal Union material while imprisoned on the island of Ventotene and it provided most of the ideas he and his small group needed to launch the Italian federal movement. He translated many Federal Union tracts into Italian as well as Lionel Robbins' *Economic Causes of War* and his *Economic Aspects of Federation*. How can this surprising phenomenon of vigorous British interest and activity concerning European federation in 1939–40 be explained?

The outbreak of war was a decisive event: considerable criticism was directed at the doctrine of state sovereignty, which it was thought prevented the League of Nations (established in 1919) from having sufficient powers to stop it. Therefore, following the defeat of Nazi Germany, a European federal structure was advocated. According to Lipgens, 'during the first year of war European federation was a central topic of debate in all sections of British opinion, whatever their (political) allegiance'. Attlee, leader of the Parliamentary Labour Party, said in 1939, 'Europe must federate or perish', and Wilson Harris, editor of the *Spectator*, wrote in March 1940, 'There is no question about the hold the idea of federal union has taken on certain sections of opinion in this country particularly ... youth.'

Pinder, while not doubting the sincerity of advocates of European federalism, thought that an element of expediency was also involved as it was discussed in the wider context of war aims between September 1939 and May 1940. The vision of a better Europe may have inspired public opinion during the 'phoney war', and helped enlist the support of the neutral US, and was even intended perhaps to weaken German support for the war (Lipgens, 1986, pp. 2–4, 23–4).

The concept of federal union was even incorporated, albeit briefly, into British government policy. The offer of complete political union between Britain and France, originally considered in March 1940, became an official government proposal from Churchill's all-party Cabinet on 16 June 1940 to create 'an indissoluble union ... not two nations but one

Franco-British Union' with joint organisations for defence, finance, foreign affairs and economic policy. The two populations would acquire a common dual citizenship. However, France collapsed the next day. Reynaud, the French prime minister, argued the case for acceptance in the French Cabinet but it was rejected by 13 votes to 11. He was ousted afterwards and a new government under Petain requested an armistice from the Germans. Churchill's offer of a Franco-British Union was intended to sustain France and its Empire in the war effort.

The fall of France in June 1940 had a formative impact on Britain's military position, her policy options and on public opinion. Discussion of federal ideas as part of war aims tailed off and the flood of publications dried up. Enthusiasm for European federalism never again achieved 1939–40 levels of interest in Britain. The talented team of researchers in the Federal Union Research Institute broke up as they became involved in war service – Beveridge to write reports on full employment and the Welfare State, and Robbins to become Head of Economic Services for the War Cabinet and later to write a report on the expansion of higher education in Britain. As Philip Bell shows, advocates of 'outright European federation' were rare in Britain between 1942–45: 'the general current of opinion had moved on' (Bell, 1986, p. 206).

It moved on because Britain's experience of war diverged from that of occupied Europe's from the summer of 1940, in two fundamental ways. First, from then until summer 1941, a period of over a year, Britain continued the war alone against Nazi Germany's European Empire. This, as Lipgens emphasises, was a formative episode as Britain's national institutions did not collapse and so the sense of national pride and independence was strengthened, unlike most of Europe's. For Britain this amounted to a triumphant vindication of reliance on and belief in national sovereignty. Furthermore, the swift collapse of continental Europe's democracies in 1939–40 served as a deterrent against any closer association with them in future.

Second, once Europe was lost, the US constituted the principal source of military aid and was to take on a special significance. While enthusiasm for European integration evaporated, the appeal of an Anglo-American Union grew. Once the USSR and US were in the war by the end of 1941, public opinion linked Britain's fate with these two emerging superpowers in 1941–45 (in contrast to the mood of 1939–40 which linked it with Europe). Their combined resources and size made eventual victory certain and also meant that these two powers would largely determine the outcome of any peace settlement (not Britain and France as it had appeared in 1939–40) (Lipgens, 1985, pp. 25–6; 1986, pp. 5–6).

After the war the British public's attention (though not the Foreign Office's, 1945–47) focused on Atlantic and world connections, and Europe was ignored. This was partly as a result of the amount of Anglo-American integration and other pieces of Anglo-American administrative apparatus established in the war, such as the US–UK Combined Chiefs of Staff and the Joint Shipping Board. It was also due to the fact that the British saw themselves as one of the 'Big Three' – the US, USSR and UK – instead of one of the big three in Europe. According to Pinder, 'the fall of France, the rise of the USA, alliance with Russia and growing hostility towards Germany combined to turn the thoughts of the British, including many Federal Unionists this way'. Lionel Robbins moved from being a champion of European Union to arguing for an Atlantic Union. Sir William Beveridge, chairman of FURI in 1940, became an advocate for the UK's association with Russia and the US in order to build a world organisation. As Pinder observed, it 'took twenty years for the wheel to come full circle and the UK to seek entry into the EEC and thirty years before it was in' (Pinder, 1986, pp. 25, 32–3).

Others, according to Lipgens, responded in a similar way to Britain. These included the neutral states (Sweden, Switzerland, Ireland, Spain and Portugal), exiles like General Charles de Gaulle and perhaps also the majority of political émigrés (there were over 1 million in Britain during the war), who had fled Europe before its conquest. All had a very different experience of the war, not being subjected to the full consequences of national collapse and subsequent rigours of totalitarian Nazi rule. Lipgens said such people 'thought that closer ties with the ruined heartland of the continent was understandably hardly urgent' and they had no reason to draw the same conclusions as those in occupied Europe where federalism at least remained an ideological force. The two groups shared a 'mutual lack of understanding' of the other's thinking after the war, in which their experience determined their position on European federation (Lipgens, 1985, pp. 25–6; 1982, pp. 58–60).

However, it was not primarily Europeans who were to decide the shape and organisational form of the post-war Continent. After 1941 it was the two continental-sized extra-European powers, the US and USSR, whose resources and manpower ensured the military defeat of Nazi Germany and – combined with the UK and the support of its Empire – ended the German occupation of Europe. Accordingly it was the evolving plans of the 'Big Three' that determined the fate of Europe. The Resistance's federalist declarations and proposals counted for nothing.

Initially (1941–42) there were two basic working themes that existed concurrently for Anglo-American post-war architecture to preserve world peace and security (although in many respects they were mutually incompatible). The first was US President Franklin D. Roosevelt's idea of two 'world policemen' in 1941 – the UK and US (by 1942 it had expanded to four 'world policemen' – the UK, US, USSR and China). The second was the idea of three regional or continental unions – including a supranational authority for Europe – upon which a world organisation could be based.

Roosevelt was shocked at the fragility of European democracies which collapsed so rapidly under the 1939–40 Nazi blitzkrieg and was disillusioned with the League of Nations which had singularly failed to preserve peace in Europe. Although not an isolationist, he initially shared their antipathy towards American involvement in any world peace organisation when the war was over, preferring to rely simply on power politics and co-operation with the UK and USSR. Roosevelt never showed any interest in promoting a European federation. Although initially the idea of some form of regional union or close association of European states was a significant component of British and American post-war planning, by the spring of 1943 the US State Department and most post-war planning commissions had broadly agreed to 'support a global peace organisation composed of continental unions'. Three such unions were envisaged among states in Asia, Europe and the Americas.

Winston Churchill, in a broadcast in March 1943, spoke along similar lines, stating that 'under a world institution of the United Nations, and some day all nations, there should come into being a Council of Europe'. The next month, April 1943, Churchill suggested a 'World Council' of the 'Big Three' with representatives of the continental unions. In May in Washington he spoke of 12 states forming a council of the 'United States of Europe'. Cordell Hull, Roosevelt's Secretary of State, basically shared Churchill's interest in a new form of the League of Nations, where small states, grouped into continental unions, would have influence as well as the big powers. Cordell Hull set up a 'Sub-Committee on the Problem of European Organisation' which met first in June 1943 and considered various plans for some months. The initiative ended with the disband-ment of this sub-committee in August 1943; any ideas for regional sub-organisations were ignored henceforth by the US as it focused on the 'world policemen' idea and creating a world organisation.

Why did this American interest in post-war Euro-federalism cease in 1943? First, the USSR under Stalin had always been opposed to any idea of federation or regional association in Europe and in 1943 Roosevelt decided to endorse this. According to Lipgens this was because, after the military feat of winning the battle for Stalingrad in 1943, the USSR carried more political and diplomatic weight in the wartime alliance of the 'Big Three'. The USSR broke off relations with governments in exile favouring federation (such as Poland) and recalled the Soviet Ambassadors from Washington and London. There were also Anglo-American suspicions and fears that the USSR had considered making a separate peace with Hitler in September 1943. For the US, after Stalingrad, the USSR had shown itself to be the 'indispensable ally' who could not be defeated (the Pentagon and White House had concluded that the US would also not be able to win a future conventional war with the USSR). Therefore Stalin's co-operation became of paramount importance to US policy for defeating Germany and securing peace after World War II.

Roosevelt tried to cultivate and placate Stalin (recognising USSR frontiers as at 22 June 1941, i.e. including annexed territory in Poland and the Baltic States) and eliminating any prospect of European federation. In return, Stalin agreed to Roosevelt's post-war plans for a United Nations Organization. The Resistance, that nursery of Euro-federalism, and organisations like the UK's Federal Union hoped rather airily to replace national sovereignty by uniting Europe in a Federal Union. But they had no influence at all on the two superpowers' policy for post-war Europe which was formally to restore nation states. Stalin had long preferred the restoration of 26 small weak European states that the USSR might then dominate. This process ultimately led to a bipolar division of Europe into two blocs in 1948–49: the Eastern Bloc centred on Moscow and the Western Bloc with its centre in Washington.

The US began to change its policy towards the USSR in 1946–47 as its perception of the USSR's intentions and reliability as a post-war partner who would adhere to agreements was re-evaluated. Soviet rule in 'liberated' Europe was extremely severe. The post-war plight of Poland meant it was saddled with a communist government imposed by Moscow. Stalin had predicted that the end of World War II would be different from other wars as the victors would impose their control over the territories they had liberated. This was at variance with the 'Declaration on Liberated Europe' that Stalin had agreed with Roosevelt and Churchill at the Yalta Conference in February 1945. This incorporated the principles of self-determination and free elections for liberated states.

The growth of East–West tension in 1946–47 shaped the emerging Anglo-American policy of dividing Germany in two, establishing a new state of West Germany (Foschepoth, 1986, pp. 404–5). After the London Conference (of the Council of Foreign Ministers from the four occupying powers) failed on 15 December 1947, this course was more firmly set. A new Bizone Agreement was in force by January 1948. Given that the earlier policy proposals of 'dismemberment' of Germany had been rejected by the US and UK and the concept of a 'united neutral Germany' was dismissed, the only option was a 'divided' Germany. This would ensure that neither superpower could incorporate an undivided big Germany within its own bloc and so upset the whole balance of power in Europe (Foschepoth, 1986, p. 406). The announcement of the Truman Doctrine to Congress on 12 March 1947 (by President Harry S. Truman who succeeded Roosevelt on his death) marked the real beginning of the Cold War between the US and USSR. Truman committed the US to the worldwide containment of communism by means of American aid to counter both communist internal insurgency and external aggression.

This was followed by the connected initiative of the Marshall Plan – the US Secretary of State, George C. Marshall, spoke of this at Harvard University on 5 June 1947. The following year a four-year programme (1948–52) of over $22 billion in American aid to 16 European states started. This was designed to assist economic recovery and lessen any prospect of communism gaining ground within Western European states. Ernest Bevin, the Labour government's Foreign Secretary 1945–51, played a significant role in precipitating this switch in US foreign policy to containment by announcing the end of all British aid to Greece, after 31 March 1947, in its fight against communist insurgents. This action culminated in the Truman Doctrine with the Americans assuming responsibility for Greece and Turkey that Britain could no longer afford. Ernest Bevin is also generally credited with turning the offer of Marshall Aid into a reality in Europe by establishing the Organization for European Economic Co-operation (OEEC) to administer it (Boyle, 1982, p. 373; Frazier, 1984, p. 715).

The start of Cold War rivalry between the superpowers – the East–West split in Europe and the division of Germany – rekindled American interest in a federal solution to Western Europe's two big problems as it would safely accommodate a revived West Germany and help to contain the USSR. After 1947 the US encouraged any promising moves towards federation or integration in Western Europe that might further the American dream of a 'United States of Europe'.

According to Lipgens, this shift in US policy encouraged the reactivation of old federalist pressure groups and the formation of new organisations advocating European union. Count Coudenhove-Kalergi revived the Pan-European Union that he had established in 1923, and in November 1946 it sent questionnaires to Western Europe's 4,000 MPs to see if they were in favour of a European federation. Fifty per cent of the Belgians, Swiss, French, Dutch and Italians, 26 per cent of the British and only 15 per cent of the Scandinavians were in favour. He then invited these MPs to participate in establishing the European Parliamentary Union, which held its first Congress at Gstaad in September 1947.

In December 1946, associations working for European federation which had their origins in Resistance movements – like Altiero Spinelli's Movimento Federalista Europeo, 1943 – met in Paris to form the Union Européenne des Fédéralistes (UEF). The Swiss 'Europa Union' and the British 'Federal Union' also joined this new transnational pressure group.

The UEF quickly recognised that the East–West split in Europe altered the practical parameters for action. The Hertenstein Programme of 1946 recognised that new geo-political realities meant the limit to any frontier of a future united Europe lay where individual liberty and personal freedom ended, thereby excluding Eastern Europe. The UEF's Montreux Congress 1947 (by then it had 100,000 members in 32 associations), agreed that while not accepting a Europe divided into two blocs as a permanent *fait accompli*, they would nevertheless try to promote federation where a start could be made in Western Europe (Lipgens, 1982, pp. 84, 585).

In addition to the PEU and UEF a rather bewildering variety of pressure groups emerged to campaign on the Euro-federal trail. All-party national organisations formed like the 'groupe parlementaire fédéraliste français' and also transnational party-affiliated pressure groups. Federalists among socialist parties from various countries created their own separate umbrella organisations, such as the 'Mouvement Socialiste pour les Etats-Unis' in 1947. (The Christian-Democrats did the same thing.)

However, arguably the most effective organisations belonged neither to the PEU nor the UEF. The UK's 'United Europe Movement' (UEM), founded by Churchill's son-in-law Duncan Sandys, had Winston Churchill (now out of office) as its president. Churchill's speech at Zurich on 19 September 1946 called for

> a kind of United States of Europe . . . [the] first step is to form a Council of Europe . . . France and Germany must take the lead together . . . - Great Britain, the British Commonwealth, mighty America – must be the friends and sponsors of the new Europe.
>
> (Lipgens, 1982, pp. 319–20)

This speech received massive publicity in the press and gave an encouraging boost to the Euro-federalist campaign. A similar body to the UEM was established in France, the 'Conseil Français pour l'Europe Uni'. A joint meeting in Paris in July 1947 led to their first joint action – a Congress at The Hague, 7–10 May 1948. Here 800 MPs, former premiers and foreign secretaries met under the chairmanship and star of the proceedings, Winston Churchill. Lipgens saw this as 'an impressive demonstration of the will to unity which formulated concrete proposals'. These included a common market, a Human Rights Convention, a European Assembly, and the transfer of a portion of states' sovereign rights to a Council of Europe.

In October 1948 the Joint International Committee of Movements for European Unity was created. This was established by the British UEM and French CFEU, and other founding organisations joined, including the UEF and transnational party-affiliated pressure groups. It adopted the name 'European Movement' under the Honorary Presidencies of Leon Blum, Winston Churchill, Alcide de Gasperi and Paul-Henri Spaak. Subsequently, following a report produced in January 1949, the Council of Europe was established by the Treaty of Westminster in May 1949 (a month after the NATO Treaty was signed). However, what was quickly agreed by the ten signatory states proved a disappointment to the European Movement's federalists. Its Parliamentary Assembly was a purely consultative body of representative national MPs (appointed by states' parliaments) and invariably those enthusiastic about creating 'Europe'. Its Committee of Ministers was the decision-making body with each foreign minister having both a vote and a veto. This was not the integrated organisation and supranational body that the Congress at The Hague had anticipated the previous year in May 1948. The Committee of Ministers moreover did not make legally binding decisions and member states chose subsequently whether to ratify agreements and conventions passed at the Council of Europe (e.g. the European Convention for the Protection of Human Rights and Fundamental Freedoms came into force in 1953. Britain was the first state to ratify it whereas France only did so in 1974).

Ernest Bevin, the UK Foreign Minister 1945–51, was reputedly instrumental in ensuring that the Council of Europe did not become an 'embarrassing organisation'. He referred to the European Movement's federalist plans for the Council of Europe as 'Pandora's box full of Trojan horses'. However, there is no evidence that any West European state was prepared idealistically to jump to political federation or union in 1948–49. This would have been a fantastic 'leap in the dark' at a time when the future of Germany had not been fully settled. So the framework of the Council of Europe in 1949 could not provide a complete answer to the German question; there were no Germans present. France was only beginning to reformulate its policy towards Germany from the summer of 1948 and only joined 'Bizonia' in April 1949 (the name for the economic fusion of UK and US occupation zones in Germany since 1947). Moreover, West European governments had many preoccupations in the late 1940s – military and economic security, dollar shortages, economic reconstruction, colonial problems and their position in the world, not just in Europe.

Paul Reynaud, longstanding French MP and ex-premier of France (1940), remarked: 'the Council of Europe consists of two bodies, one of them for Europe, the other against it' – the latter being the Committee of Ministers. Even Paul-Henri Spaak, the Belgian Prime Minister, who was one of the most 'federally' minded statesmen in office, was primarily motivated by the understandable need to enhance Belgium's own military and economic security (Milward, 1992, pp. 320–4).

For many idealistic Euro-federalists in the European Movement it must have seemed in 1948–49 that everything was coming together in Western Europe. They were encouraged in this both by the USSR's threatening behaviour (the Soviet blockade of West Berlin and the Anglo-American airlift to overcome it – flying in coal, food and clothing for ten and a half months, finally ending on 12 May 1949) and by the start of Marshall Aid from the US, administered through the OEEC. (From June 1948 $22.4 billion was granted over four years for European reconstruction.) The Americans hoped that the OEEC could be developed into a Customs Union for Western Europe (see next chapter). The NATO Treaty was signed in April 1949, creating a permanent peacetime military alliance (initially planned for 20 years) with national forces assigned to its integrated command structure. It established a North Atlantic Council and an Executive Committee of Foreign Ministers, a Defence Council of War Ministers and a Committee of Chiefs of Staff. It was signed by the original five Brussels Treaty Organisation States – Britain, France, Belgium, Holland, Luxembourg – and by the US, Canada, Italy, Portugal, Iceland, Denmark and Norway. General Eisenhower became NATO's first supreme commander until he was elected American President in 1952. NATO was very much a consequence of the first big Cold War crisis of the Berlin Blockade 1948–49.

So in 1949 it doubtless appeared for many representatives in the Parliamentary Assembly a highly propitious moment to push for political federation in the Council of Europe, given the formation of NATO and the possibility of a European Customs Union forming, with American encouragement, out of the OEEC. However, this apparent window of opportunity was barred, as was demonstrated during the first session of the Council of Europe in November 1949 in Strasbourg, France (a venue suggested by Ernest Bevin, given its symbolic location on the border of

France and Germany – and the fact that it had changed hands four times since 1870). According to Lipgens this session had a 'humiliating outcome' as federalists in the Council of Europe tried to modify the Treaty of Westminster. The British and Scandinavians on the Committee of Ministers vetoed all such federalist recommendations from the Parliamentary Assembly. The move to European federation through changing the 1949 Statute of the Council of Europe was blocked.

It was ironic that the only European organisation that can be attributed directly to the European Movement's influence was not an integrated or supranational body. Nevertheless the UEF saw the Council of Europe as the start of 'a real organic co-operation between European States'. It has also been described as 'an important milestone on the road to the closer association of the European community' (Urwin, 1991, p. 39).

However, the Council of Europe and its institutions are quite distinct and separate from those created for the supranational ECSC and EEC. The European Community's European Parliament, Commission, Council of Ministers, European Court of Justice and most confusingly European Council (the biannual heads of state meeting) have nothing whatever to do with the Council of Europe's Parliamentary Assembly, Committee of Ministers, European Commission of Human Rights and European Court of Human Rights. The Council of Europe and the European Community are completely separate bodies formed from very different motivations and for different purposes.

The Council of Europe has produced over 140 European conventions since 1949 notably on human rights, on the prevention of torture, and on the suppression of terrorism. One of the Council of Europe's primary concerns has been the enhancement and protection of human rights in Europe. This was a major objective of Euro-federalists given Nazi atrocities, genocide and the wholesale violation of human rights during 1933–45. Since 1949 the original ten members have grown to 26, with Hungary, Poland and Czechoslovakia joining in 1990–91. Member states must accept the principle of the rule of law and guarantee that everyone under its jurisdiction enjoys their human rights and fundamental freedoms. The Council of Europe is not concerned with economic issues at all.

The only connection between the Council of Europe and the European Community is that the EC's European Parliament holds its plenary sessions at the Council of Europe's Palais de l'Europe in Strasbourg. Also, since May 1986 when EC membership reached 12 states, the EC adopted the Council of Europe's flag as its official emblem. The familiar 12 gold stars on a blue background has been the Council of

Europe's flag since 1955; the 12 stars are apparently 'an invariable number symbolising perfection and entirety' (Council of Europe, 1992, p. 15).

Although the Council of Europe is invariably described as a first step or milestone on the road to a closer Europe, in a sense it has been bypassed by the creation of the supranational ECSC and EEC. The evidence suggests that the Council of Europe, despite its disappointing limitations for Euro-federalists, represented not only the highpoint but also a dead-end for organised European federalist movements' influence.

Individual federalists and converts like Jean Monnet (who invented the ECSC's High Authority) and Robert Schuman, the French Foreign Minister, made an immense contribution to European economic integration in the early 1950s. Federalists continued to exercise influence long after this. A group founded by Alterio Spinelli in the European Parliament, called 'the crocodile club', was responsible for initiating the parliaments' draft Treaty on European Union in 1982 (Wallace, 1982, p. 67, n.24). Nevertheless, as an organised idealistic movement that grew in the wartime resistance and was revived in 1946–47, the European federalist movements' pinnacle of achievement was the Council of Europe.

Creating the Council of Europe in 1949 certainly meant that the European Movement focused its attention there in vain attempts to steer it in a more federal direction in 1949–50. The European Parliamentary Union's third and fourth Congresses in 1949 and 1950 were almost wholly devoted to a critique of the Council of Europe's structure and debates (Lipgens, 1980, p. 129). Yet only six months after the Council of Europe's first session in November 1949, the Schuman Plan in May 1950 (leading to the ECSC) and the Pleven Plan in October 1950 (leading to the EDC scheme) were formally proposed by the French government. Despite assertions to the contrary, there are no signs of any notable direct involvement by European federalist movements on either scheme.

So what was the significance of the European federalist movements? They were clearly an interesting phenomenon and subsequent developments in the 1950s demonstrated the opportune relevance and inherent logic of some of their recommendations – such as a Customs Union or a common market. Even though their campaign for a European federation failed, the campaign indicated at the very least that there was a more widely recognised need for a new structure and architecture in post-war Europe. However, problems surrounding plans for Europe did not arise with the European federalists' prime activities of formulating and advocating ideal policy options but in actually agreeing and implementing mutually satisfactory arrangements between states. Governments were only motivated to do this (see Chapter 3) by way of solving difficulties affecting specific national economic interests. They were not seduced by Euro-federal idealism but driven, as Milward argued, by the need to find the appropriate international framework both to maintain national economic recovery and to solve the German question. National interest, not Euro-federal idealism, propelled the schemes for economic integration. The ECSC and EEC were the result of lengthy detailed negotiating and bargaining between six West European states.

The European federalist movement is probably accorded too much importance and its role as a force exaggerated in the development of integrated organisations. Even the supposedly influential Hertenstein Conference of September 1946 organised by Dutch and Swiss federalists did not manage to contact the British Federal Union and other groups. These then held their own separate Luxembourg conference in October 1946, to which the Dutch and Swiss were not invited – apparently because their addresses had been lost! (Lipgens, 1982, p. 303). Although the 'Hertenstein programme' was adopted subsequently as the manifesto for most Euro-federal groups, there were only 78 people at this conference and 41 of those were Swiss. Both conferences were concerned as much with world federation as European and received little publicity 'in the ordinary press ... The Hertenstein and Luxembourg conference received, at most, a brief inconspicuous mention' (Lipgens, 1982, p. 317).

It was Winston Churchill's Zurich speech on 19 September 1946, that really energised the campaign for federation in Europe by the publicity it received.

Where does this leave Lipgens' thesis? Lipgens thought that the 'progress of the movement for European Union was comparable with that of Liberal democracy in the 19th century', in so far as over a long period of time the movement began with individuals and writers and extended to national and transnational pressure groups which eventually affected the political elites. Then governments 'increasingly affected by the idea started to put it partially into effect' (Lipgens, 1982, p. vi). This is rather dubious, particularly as governments that were unenthusiastic about political federation in Europe in 1949 were attracted by economic integration in 1950. Nevertheless, Lipgens assumes that the inevitable outcome of economic integration is federal union and therefore whatever gets established is simply a means to that end, not an end in itself. The reality though was that France, Belgium, Holland and Britain still had substantial imperial interests and responsibilities in the late 1940s and 1950s. However, Lipgens surprisingly asserts that 'their sense of being colonial powers prevented these countries in the first decisive years of the European integration movement from understanding what had become inevitable' (Lipgens, 1982, p. 12).

The effectiveness of European federalist movements was probably reduced as a result of the schisms in the movement – experienced in 1949 with the disappointments surrounding the Council of Europe and the setback in 1954 when the EDC collapsed. This was due to ideological disputes (the UEF was 'torn apart over future strategy' in 1954) or to personality clashes among the leadership (the EPU split in 1949 was a result of this). Lipgens mentions that after 1954 the European Movement lost its impetus and ceased to be very active or influential (Lipgens, 1980, p. 137).

How influential were the leaders of European federalist movements before this? Some were highly prominent, well-known and even famous, revered figures like Winston Churchill who was out of government on the opposition benches between 1945–51, and consequently powerless at the time. Many more though were 'hommes d'affairs' who were really 'playing at being influential' (Watt, 1980, p. 109). Moreover, it is conceivable that the European federal movements' campaign might have encouraged or engendered attitudes and organisations opposed to European federation. Certainly in France two big parties, the Gaullist RPF on the right, and the communists on the left, were implacably hostile. In Britain 'ties of kinship with the Commonwealth, were obviously an important counter-influence' (Lipgens, 1982, p. 196).

Lipgens' attempt to attribute the phenomenon of European economic integration of the 1950s to the influence of the European federalist movements' campaign in the 1940s largely ignores the crucial experience of governments' failures in international policy-making in the 1920s and 1930s. The fact is that the late 1940s and 1950s were not the first time that a Franco-German economic rapprochement had been attempted or the problem of access to European raw materials tackled through international organisations. After World War I there was an attempt to maintain wartime allied co-operation in raw materials through a Supreme Economic Council, established in February 1919, which intended to try to ensure an adequate supply of raw materials for the devastated areas. This body was incapacitated by having too limited a remit and inadequate powers and authority to deal with the distribution of raw materials. In August 1919 a European Coal Commission was created to co-ordinate coal production and distribution in Europe but it too lacked sufficient authority (Aldcroft, 1977, pp. 60–1). A Franco-German rapprochement based on a bilateral agreement for coal and steel was developed by the

French in the mid-1920s and led to the steel cartel and the short-lived Franco-German Commercial Treaty of August 1927 (McDougall, 1978, pp. 372–4). These and other attempts at international co-operation were wrecked ultimately by the world economic depression of 1929–32. This encouraged protectionism and economic nationalism, i.e. purely national attempts to solve what were international problems (the over-production of world agriculture, surplus capacity in industry, falling prices and export earnings for many countries, and world financial instability), all of which were only solvable through international co-operation.

A basic weakness of the international and European economy in the 1920s and 1930s was the failure to develop international policies which would be adhered to once agreed. The problem was that regulation and enforcement of policy was left almost entirely in national control.

So, as Aldcroft states, 'International efforts to promote reconstruction were woefully inadequate after the First World War, a lesson which was appreciated by the planners responsible for the same tasks after 1945' (Aldcroft, 1977, p. 63). The eventual emergence of schemes for European economic integration, starting significantly with coal and steel, must be seen in the context of the previous post-war experience of failure in the 1920s. Unsuccessful agreements in the 1920s, such as the short-lived Franco-German Commercial Treaty of 1927, demonstrated that something more authoritative, permanent and law-abiding had to be devised for commercial agreements post-1945. The eventual solution of a supranational Customs Union and common market for coal and steel had its origins (as the next chapter shows) in the deliberations of the European Customs Union Study Group 1947–49.

# Chapter 3

# Conditions in Europe and American and British policies, 1945–49
## Integration or co-operation?

Western Europe's political and economic position and military security looked precarious in 1945–47. Agricultural output in 1946–47 was only 75 per cent of the 1938 level; a UN Commission estimated in 1946 that 100 million Europeans lived on less than 1,500 calories per day (i.e. they were going hungry). In the UK, bread and potatoes were rationed from mid-1946 – not during the war itself – to enable supplies to be sent to the British Military Zone in Germany. In 1947, industrial production in Belgium, Netherlands and France was still 30–40 per cent lower than in 1939. European conditions were made worse in 1946–47 by a wet summer and a severe winter leading to poor harvests and a fuel crisis as snow disrupted coal supplies. There were massive shortages of fuel, food and industrial capital goods (Germany had been eliminated as the main pre-war supplier of the latter); this meant a large trading deficit with the US as the alternative supplier, and a dollar shortage.

Governments were faced with a severe fall in foreign trade (the UK's trade was only 70 per cent of the pre-war level in 1946–47) and were threatened with inflation (prices were driven up by shortages) and the need to increase exports well above pre-war levels. Nevertheless, despite such evidence, Western Europe's economic recovery from this austere state was already remarkably swift, assisted by Marshall Aid, which provided a marked increase in capital goods imports from the US between 1947–52. The recovery was sustained as a long boom through the 1950s and 1960s. Between 1948–50 annual sales of washing machines grew from 94,000 to 311,000 in the UK and from 20,000 to 100,000 in France. By 1950 Western Europe's foreign trade was already 20 per cent above pre-war levels and production was rising every year.

The political situation in post-war Europe was also potentially chaotic. Reinstated national governments (many of which spent 1940–45 in exile in London) were faced with danger from gunmen. The UK had armed communist and non-communist resistance forces in the war. Fifty thousand Sten guns had been dropped and, in wartime, killing military and political opponents was sanctioned, a habit which tended to persist into peacetime as old scores were settled. After liberating each state, the Western Allies tried to disarm the Resistance quickly to avoid the danger of reinstated authorities being overturned by communist or other gunmen in Western Europe, as occurred in Greece in 1944.

The Communist Party also increased its strength in Western Europe after the war (even though only 10 per cent of Resistance forces were communist) because of widespread sympathy for the USSR and its war effort between 1941–44 (it lost between 20–40 million civilians and service personnel and killed 3 million German troops). Post-war governments in France, Belgium and Italy included Communist Party ministers up to 1947. Moscow's Cominform in 1947 meant that the USSR exercised control over Western Europe's Communist Parties which duly took Moscow's side in the Cold War. In 1947–48 numerous communist-led strikes in France, Italy and Britain (notably in the docks) were essentially protests against economic hardship and the high cost of living that were exploited by the Communist Parties and the USSR.

Liberation brought exaggerated hopes and expectations. This, combined with the political and economic disruption of the first 18 months of peace, created a dangerous situation. It was in this context that the USA's offer of Marshall Aid was made in 1947. As Ernest Bevin, the British Labour Government's Foreign Minister 1945–51, confessed this offer seemed 'like a life-line to sinking men'.

The end of the war and the end of the common enemy meant the collapse of the war-time Grand Alliance of the 'Big Three'. The US had not abandoned its 'one world' efforts to reach agreement with the USSR over Germany, Eastern Europe and elsewhere and it reduced its troop strength in Western Europe very rapidly from 3.5 million in June 1945 to 200,000 by June 1947; even at the end of 1945 Britain had 488,000 stationed in Germany compared with 390,000 American troops. This showed that America had not accepted any permanent military commitment to European defence after 1945.

Many aspects of the wartime special relationship with Britain were quickly ended by President Truman in September 1945, including the Anglo-American administrative machinery such as the combined Chiefs of Staff Committee. The atomic partnership was also scrapped, despite being enshrined in the Quebec Agreement of August 1943 and the Hyde Park Memorandum of September 1944. Technical co-operation had ceased by April 1946 and the McMahon Act of August 1946 stopped any further exchanges of nuclear information. This setback meant that from January 1947 Britain started its own atomic weapons programme. As Bevin told the Cabinet Committee authorising it, 'We've got to have this thing over here, whatever it costs . . . we've got to have the bloody Union Jack flying on top of it.'

The USA's swift withdrawal from Europe in 1945 took place as the USSR appeared menacing and remained in strength. This meant that Britain (Europe's only undefeated power) bore the main burden of European security against the USSR in the mid-1940s. This accounts for the renewed genuine enthusiasm between 1945–48 for Western European co-operation and unity by the British government. To the Foreign Office, American policy and action over their European commitments in 1945 began to resemble the post-World War I experience. Then the US had reverted to a more isolationist position – like 'the great betrayal' of 1919–20 when it failed to join the League of Nations which it had largely created. The fact that American military assistance could not be relied upon meant that the Foreign Office's aspiration for a 'Western Bloc' was enthusiastically pursued by Bevin. Drawing Western European states together would enhance their mutual security and might also serve to strengthen the UK's world position *vis-à-vis* the US and the USSR by building up Britain as 'the great European power' (according to Sir Orme Sargent, Permanent Secretary at the Foreign Office, October 1945).

In 1946 Germany was still the principal security problem for the French, who feared a revanchist Germany. Bevin was instrumental in creating an Anglo-French peacetime alliance under the Treaty of Dunkirk on 4 March 1947.

In the absence of a firm permanent American commitment to European defence between 1945–47, Bevin took the lead in creating a 'Western Bloc' for European security. Moreover, in doing this, he hoped to convince the Americans that Europeans were working closely together to defend themselves and that because of the threat from the militarily powerful USSR, the US should become directly involved in European defence. Bevin's objective in 1947–48 was to draw together the western powers, including the US, into a political, economic and military bloc, with the US becoming directly involved in Western Europe's defence. Bevin played a significant role in precipitating a volte-face in US foreign policy with the Truman Doctrine and the announcement of Marshall Aid by declaring Britain's termination of military aid to Greece and Turkey.

To suggest that Bevin simply played up the Russian threat to get American financial aid is exaggerated. It is also wrong to think that containment was a policy hatched in Washington and imposed on a reluctant Europe in exchange for Dollar Aid. The initiative for containment really came from the UK. Foreign Office papers show the Labour government from 1945 pursuing a policy of firmer resistance towards the USSR than the capitalist US. Frazier (1984) sees it as an inspired stroke of statesmanship: 'Bevin's action in 1947 had to a significant extent been responsible for the Truman Doctrine and the policy of containment' (Frazier, 1984, pp. 725–6). Boyle (1982) argues that the western response of the Truman Doctrine and Marshall Aid to the Soviet threat was

> neither a policy hatched in Washington and imposed on Europe nor a policy conceived in London which the US was lured into accepting. It was a policy towards which the US had been moving . . . with more hesitation and vagaries than are sometimes appreciated. Britain played a role in drawing America towards such a policy.
>
> (Boyle, 1982, p. 389)

The details of containment were discussed and settled between the two states and with Canada and Western Europe.

The American Secretary of State, General George C. Marshall made his Harvard speech on 5 June 1947 in which he proposed a plan for the economic recovery of Europe. Bevin reported to Parliament on 19 June, 'When the Marshall proposals were announced, I grabbed them with both hands' (Kirby, 1977, pp. 96–7). Bevin's enthusiastic response and initiative made the US offer of aid a reality. Washington's aim was to use Dollar Aid as a lever to create a more economically and politically integrated Western Europe (but without clear plans for implementing this). By bringing the 'European Recovery Programme' (ERP) into existence Bevin played the leading role creating the 16-nation Committee of European Economic Co-operation (CEEC) Paris Conference in the summer of 1947, chaired by Sir Oliver Franks, to discuss the Marshall Aid programme. Out of this was created the Organization for European Economic Co-operation (OEEC), a year later in 1948, chaired by Sir Edmund Hall-Patch. Within the OEEC Britain conceived an inter-European payment scheme.

As early as 1946 Bevin had asked the Foreign Office to consider the possibility of an Anglo-French Customs Union that others might join later. During the CEEC discussions the Customs Union idea came to the fore. The British delegation proposed the establishment of a Customs Union Study Group (CUSG) to meet in Brussels, and so away from American pressure in Paris, to consider the whole question of a Western European Customs Union from 1947. In September 1947 at the TUC Conference

Bevin envisaged a Customs Union with members retaining their Imperial Preferences.

By February 1948 Bevin and the Foreign Office 'had fully espoused the cause of a West European Customs Union'. On 22 January 1948 Bevin announced to Parliament in his 'Western Union speech' that 'We are thinking now of Western Europe as a unity. . . we should do all we can to advance the spirit and machinery of cooperation' (House of Commons Debates, 23 January 1948, vol. 466, col. 397). Bevin and the Foreign Office saw the strong case for a Western European Customs Union lying in its political, military and strategic advantages. A closer association among Western European states was considered essential for security. To Bevin, a Customs Union was not just desirable but a necessary basis for a West European defensive alliance and was given a high foreign policy priority in order to halt 'the flow of the Communist tide'. The Foreign Office motives were purely political, while the UK's economic ministries flatly rejected the idea and so a divide existed between the perceived economic disadvantages and the political advantages.

The Board of Trade feared that the UK steel and chemicals industries would require permanent protection once the limits on the volume of German industrial production were removed. The Treasury was concerned as Britain's reserves were also the Sterling Area's reserves and should not be endangered in any way as this could jeopardise the UK's and the world's recovery. There was a deep suspicion of American policy designs and of their Customs Union idea as a means to attack the position of the City of London and grab its 'invisible business' for New York. However, Bevin was reluctant to abandon the idea of a Customs Union linked to Imperial Preferences (including the Empire and the Commonwealth trade) as a way to independence from the US in January 1948 (Milward, 1984, p. 245).

In the face of opposition from economic ministries in Britain, 'Bevin let the matter drop, overtaken as it was by the spread of alternative defence structures in the Brussels Pact and NATO' (Milward, 1982, pp. 550–1). As Milward says, in retrospect the UK's decision not to participate in the formation of the first proposed West European Customs Union in 1948 was 'a vital moment in British history when a wrong turning was taken . . . and everyone involved was aware of being faced with a historical choice of great moment'.

The unanimous opinion of civil servants and those economists consulted was that a Customs Union would 'automatically lead to much closer forms of political union and necessarily to the wholesale harmonisation of economic policies in Europe which in 1945–47 varied enormously'. The UK's political and administrative elite saw the Customs Union idea as a major irreversible shift in policy. So the appeal of the status quo in 1948 seemed extremely comforting. This alternative option also looked more than sound as the UK still had semi-Great Power status with a global military spread, the Sterling Area and worldwide trade connections (Milward, 1982, p. 551; 1984, pp. 236–7). Bevin let the issue drop in the face of economic ministries' objections and because it appeared from available advice that a Customs Union would inevitably restrain the UK's freedom of action in other areas.

Bevin's notion of West European unity was eventually based on co-operation in interdependent organisations rather than unity through integration in supranational organisations. He had a vision of a 'trans-Atlantic Western Union' and this policy started to take shape when Britain, France and the Benelux countries signed the Brussels Treaty of economic, social and cultural collaboration and collective self-defence on 17 March 1948 (the Brussels Pact 1948), thereby creating the 'Western Union'. Bevin was interested in strategic issues here, economic arrangements to him were mainly for ancillary support. Under Article 4, a Western Union Defence Organization was established with Headquarters at Fontainebleau in September 1948 and Field Marshal Montgomery became first chairman of the Chiefs of Staff of the Western Union – all of which symbolised Britain's new and strong commitment to the defence of Europe. However, this was a Europe of independent states co-operating together, not a federation.

Once the Brussels Pact was established, Bevin and the Foreign Office let the issue of a Customs Union drop from April 1948, although this was not announced until January 1949 as being official policy and discussions within the CUSG continued.

Bevin constantly pressed for greater US military commitment. The ultimate motive here was that once Britain had sorted out European defence and obtained a US commitment to Europe, it could then get on with its own affairs in the world. In this, Bevin was helped by the USSR's extremely inept foreign policy, such as the stage-managed Prague coup of February 1948, the USSR's pressure on Norway in March 1948 and the start of the blockade of West Berlin in June 1948 – all of which served to accelerate American military commitments to Western Europe. US Senate Resolution 239 allowed the US government to become involved in 'collective arrangements for defence' in June 1948 and by July 1948, 60 American B29 atom bombers were operating from East Anglian airfields. The NATO Treaty signed on 4 April 1949 owed much to the work of Bevin and Sir Oliver Franks (the *deus ex machina* of British government administration in the 1940s and 1950s). For Bevin, the realisation of a vision of a transatlantic Western Union was his crowning foreign policy achievement. The UK's commitment to European defence was now encased in an expanded North Atlantic context more in keeping with Britain's maritime and global traditions.

NATO, in reality, until the outbreak of the Korean War in June 1950 was a 'paper treaty' as members were more concerned with their economic recovery than with rearmament.

The Americans in 1947 expected the UK to take the lead in organising Europe and to bring it to political and economic unity. Bevin accomplished this in his own way through the Brussels Pact. Such co-operation fell short of the vague American objective of a Customs Union and Federation. Bevin seriously considered creating a Customs Union including the British Empire between 1947–48 mainly for strategic purposes. He was motivated to do this and take the lead in Europe given the absence of any permanent American commitment to European defence between 1945–49. The British were criticised for not doing more to create European unity, supposedly denying the Council of Europe in 1949 and also the OEEC supranational authority. British officials saw this accusation as 'a great injustice', given Britain's initiative in establishing the OEEC, Brussels Pact and NATO. As Edwin Playfair, a Treasury official wrote, 'In the OEEC, the easiest alibi . . . is to put forward a resolution that the moon be dragged out of the sea with nets and say the British blocked it' (Boyle, 1982, p. 383).

As far as Britain was concerned its only acknowledged 'fault' was that it did not immediately and unthinkingly accept the more grandiose schemes for European union, especially some of the 'wilder American bright ideas'.

With the return of Churchill's Conservative government to power in 1951–55, European-minded ministers and MPs ('Tory Strasbourgers') portrayed Bevin and the Labour government as 'anti-European'. This was not in fact the case at all between 1945–49, it was simply that Bevin's prescriptions and designs were ultimately based upon co-operation – interdependent organisations rather than supranational bodies that the US wanted and which the French between 1948–49 were coming to see as essential. The difference between French and British policies on Europe were determined by their different national interests. For France, European interests were their top priority (the German problem dominated attention). For the UK, by 1948–49, European issues were not the foremost concern. Britain's global economic and military interests took precedence (Young, 1984, pp. x, 180–6) because, by 1949, the US commitment to NATO meant that Europe was more secure from the USSR and that Britain was not the only power shouldering the burden of containing it and organising European defence and co-operation.

Besides, Britain's foreign policy largely followed her economic interests and only 25 per cent of Britain's trade was with Europe in the 1950s – which was actually lower than in the 1930s.

In fact, the period 1948–49 – rather like 1940 – was a pivotal moment in British and French history regarding the formulation of their respective European policies. A major rethink in Britain's policy towards Europe was conducted in Whitehall on 5 January 1949 which finally rejected the Customs Union idea, the Foreign Office coming round to the Treasury and Board of Trade's point of view. The US realised from then on that the UK could not be dragooned into economic integration with Europe. This Whitehall meeting decided that within the Atlantic Pact 'we hope to secure a special relationship with the US and Canada . . . economic recovery depends not on structural reforms such as federation but on American aid'. The criterion for Britain's continental commitment by October 1949 was 'limited liability' (the same slogan as was used by military planners in the 1930s). What this meant was that Britain was prepared to assist European recovery but at the same time would be careful that such assistance would not weaken Britain so it ceased to be a worthwhile ally to America, should Europe ever collapse. The Treasury and Foreign Office clearly stated that Britain's ties with America and the Commonwealth 'take priority over our relations with Europe' (Reynolds, 1988, p. 235; Young, 1984, pp. 127–31).

The fact that France was politically and economically weak in 1949 whilst the US had renewed its association with Europe through Marshall Aid and NATO meant that an unprecedented peacetime alliance was forming. Dean Acheson, US Secretary of State, described this period of Cold War diplomacy as 'being present at the creation'.

Meanwhile France, having involved itself in the CUSG, saw a Customs Union from the summer of 1948 as the way forward for the reconstruction of Western Europe, especially as a West German state began to re-emerge and German economic recovery commenced during 1947–48 (although more slowly than its neighbours).

According to Milward, 1949 was also a watershed commercially and economically. In 1948 only Britain and Switzerland had higher exports than in 1938. In 1946 Britain's total value of foreign trade was 45 per cent of Western Europe's as a whole and even in 1950 it was still 33 per cent, yet Britain had balance of payments crises and experienced devaluations in 1947 and 1949. In 1949 the long-expected post-war American recession occurred (just as the experience after World War I was a restocking boom, 1919–20, followed by a severe economic collapse in 1920–21). In fact, the US recession was very mild and short-lived. US exports were maintained by the policies of Marshall Aid and rearmament. Nevertheless, the US recession caused a fall in American imports from the rest of the world. The British economy was the main casualty, Britain's dollar earnings were hit and the dollar position of the Sterling Area reserves was damaged by the US recession. Britain's worldwide exports were adversely affected, causing a balance of payments crisis that in turn led to a sterling crisis and a 30 per cent devaluation of sterling against the dollar on 18 September 1949.

Significantly, Western Europe was not adversely affected by the American recession. Western Europe's export boom continued. It was insulated from the US recession of 1948–49 because of the timing of the West German economic recovery which sucked in imports from France, Holland and Belgium and caused export-led growth in Western Europe which continued to dominate the 1950s boom. Britain's exports stagnated relative to Europe's because of its geographical distribution of exports, concentrated in the slow-growing Commonwealth markets. The UK was already excluding itself from the benefits of dynamic West European trade. Although French output stagnated in 1949, her exports increased considerably, according to Milward's research, because of West Germany's growth and this convinced the French that a more liberal trade framework was useful.

Whereas Britain's exports to 'Little Europe' increased by 38 per cent between 1948–50, the exports of these six states to each other increased by 90 per cent (Milward, 1984, pp. 337–9). This showed the weakness of Britain's position for the future, in the 1950s and 1960s. Britain's distribution of exports was ignoring the fastest-growing market of Western Europe and focusing on South Africa and the Commonwealth which were growing more slowly and were more susceptible to volatile fluctuations in the American economy and, in the case of Australia and New Zealand, they introduced import substitution policies to foster their own industries, so curbing British exports.

The 1949 crisis showed the potential health of Western Europe's market and trading system compared with Britain's position. Until 1949 the Labour government, as Milward shows, could have reconstructed Europe its way – with a Customs Union including Imperial Preference – but they turned away from that to 'limited liability' on Europe and renewing the 'special relationship'.

Milward argues that the movement of foreign trade in Western Europe

1949–50 produced a radical alteration in the scope for political action there. It weakened Britain's position and influence and strengthened that of France. For France in 1947, forming a Customs Union in Europe without Britain was inconceivable and even dangerous. However, with the emergence of the Federal Republic of Germany in May 1948 as both a political entity and a reviving economy – with a boom in German trade in 1949 – a Customs Union was now seen by France and also Holland (even without UK participation) as realistic and essential. Previously, industrial production was strictly controlled by the Western Allies and West Germany was not in the OEEC. West Germany's rapid economic recovery 1949–50 meant an expanding export market for its neighbours – principally Holland and France. French industrial output in fact stagnated in 1949 – the domestic economy was not expanding – yet French exports to the FRG continued to grow vigorously. For the Dutch and the French, a Customs Union appeared a political and economic necessity in 1948–49.

The British Foreign Office wrongly assumed in 1949 that a Customs Union without Britain was unlikely to emerge – in fact, the reverse was probably true, as it was arguably easier to negotiate and arrange with Britain absent in 1950.

The US in 1949 abandoned any hope that the UK would take the lead in integrating Europe. This gave France her opportunity to create an international framework for European reconstruction that suited French interests and was acceptable to other West European states, rather than reflecting American wishes. The US vision was of a large liberal free-trade unified Europe of the 16 OEEC countries, whereas the emerging French scheme of 1949–50 was of a small, closely regulated market – a 'Little Europe' of six states. As in the 1920s, coal and steel remained the central issue in reconstructing Franco-German economic and political relations – the Customs Union and common market in coal and steel of the Schuman Plan June 1950 was the outcome. The route to this scheme was via discussions in the CUSG between 1947–49 with France seriously considering the Customs Union solution to its 'German problem' from the summer of 1948 – as the FRG began to emerge after the London Conference in July 1948. The three military governments of the Western Zone of Germany handed over the 'Frankfurt Documents' to the Minister-Presidents of 11 West German states, calling for a constituent assembly and a parliamentary council. In May 1949 the 'Basic Law' (the FRG's constitution) was decreed and ratified and on 21 September 1949 the three military governments of the Western Zones – British, American and French – handed over the 'Occupation Statutes' granting West

Germany full legal, executive and judicial powers (though not over foreign policy or defence matters until later in 1955). In this way, West Germany's capacity for self-government was created and its sovereignty granted in stages. The first Bundestag elections were held on 14 August 1949, Konrad Adenauer was elected as the first Federal-Chancellor on 20 September 1949 and on 28 October 1949 the FRG was admitted to the OEEC (the exception to the rule that the FRG could not control its own foreign affairs).

September 1948 to September 1949 was a 'turning point', as so much was changing in these 12 months. There were many elements that coincided: the Berlin airlift, the formation of NATO and the American military commitment to Europe, the Cold War and the consequent complete division of Europe into East–West Blocs ('two big dogs chewing on a bone' as US Senator Fulbright described it), the re-emergence of the West German state, the sterling crisis of 1949 and the Whitehall policy rethink in January 1949, a policy which continued with Churchill's government in 1951–55. The West German economic recovery in 1949 focused French attention and converted the Netherlands to a 'French style' regulated Customs Union solution for Germany. The US gave up the idea of the OEEC path to integrating Europe in 1949 and abandoned the idea that the UK was going to lead the way to an integrated Europe. The US saw the UK more as an ally in financial trouble, rather than a trading rival. Moreover, with the UK's global military and economic commitments, Britain was an essential junior partner in the US containment of Soviet communism.

Britain had long enjoyed an ambivalent relationship with both the US and Western Europe. Despite ties of language, culture and people, the UK and US were locked into a '*competitive cooperation*' (Reynolds, 1980, pp. 233–45). When faced with a dangerous common threat (as with Hitler's Germany 1939–45 and Stalin's USSR post-1948) a 'special relationship' developed. This was a deliberate act of policy by the UK from January 1949 and relations became very close as the UK and her Commonwealth were vital to the Cold War containment of the USSR. In fact, the UK was not really treated as a foreign country by the US State Department by the early 1950s. Acheson, US Secretary of State, and UK Ambassador Franks, had weekly, two-hour, wide-ranging conversations.

The UK's foreign relations towards Europe had traditionally followed the 'balance of power' doctrine: namely, the weight of diplomacy was thrown against any new European power bloc (whether Napoleon I, Napoleon III, Tsarist Russia, the Kaiser, Hitler, the USSR, or even arguably the EEC 1956–60 [because of the threat of a Franco-German 'superstate']). However, given the absence of a US military defence commitment to Europe in the immediate post-war years (1945–48), the UK – primarily for strategic reasons – was forced to take the lead in organising collective defence and other co-operative measures to re-inforce this (such as exploring the Customs Union idea). So the hiatus of US commitment meant that the UK became more 'European' in its approach during 1945–48. Once the US was committed to European recovery and defence, the UK was able to revert to a policy of 'limited liability' and a more 'semi-detached' position by 1949 – European integration should not be encouraged as the US could leave if it was effective. The British Foreign Office arguably took far too short-term a view – it did not try to look 10–15 years ahead. It lacked vision and long-term objectives and practised 'shopkeeper' or 'mercantile' diplomacy (as opposed to Robert Schuman's bold 'heroic diplomacy'). This meant simply dealing with things as they turned up, not thinking about the future; it meant compromise via negotiation and fair dealing between rivals, not beating them (Schlain et al., 1977, p. 89). The UK was mainly preoccupied by its global military/trade relations, decolonisation and relations with the newly independent states.

What motivated US policy on Europe with Marshall Aid from 1947? Marshall Aid was motivated by America's fear of Europe's impending collapse, economically and then politically. The hard winter of 1947 interrupted British production of steel, coal and manufactured goods. In France agricultural production suffered as wheat was killed by a hard winter followed by spring floods and drought in summer. American reports in 1947 on the state of Europe were extremely pessimistic. The US feared that this would produce a windfall political gain for the USSR's influence (via support for the Communist Party in Europe) and also an economic slump in the US, as its exports to Europe would suffer. The 'Cleveland–Moore–Kindleberger' Memorandum of 12 June 1947 on the ERP emphasised that: 'the heart of the European problem is inadequate production' (Kindleberger, 1987, p. 9). In fact, although conditions were chaotic and economic and political systems weakened post-war, recovery (though only post-1947 in West Germany) was under way from 1945. To Americans, Europe, with its visible austerity, was very poor compared with the US – per capita income was lower in 1946 than in 1938 whereas the USA's had risen by 25 per cent.

Post-war Europe suffered from an acute dollar shortage and the USA's fear in spring 1947 was that European recovery might stop because of a lack of dollars, and given that US industrial capacity had grown so much because of its World War II expansion (as the 'arsenal for democracy') that

US output and employment would suffer badly (US industrial labour force grew from 10 million to 17 million in 1940–44). Europe's balance of payments deficit was rising rapidly from $5.8bn in 1946 to $7.5bn in 1947 as compared with an approximate balance in 1938. Paradoxically, this was both problematic but also a clear sign of European economic recovery. Germany had traditionally been Western Europe's main supplier of capital goods exports (machinery and vehicles); with the defeat and military occupation of Germany it was eliminated as a supplier. The US remained the only large alternative source of capital goods for Western Europe given that the UK concentrated on trade with the Commonwealth and Sterling Area.

The wide US trade surplus in 1947 – exporting $16bn goods, importing only $8bn goods – meant that Europe found it very hard to earn dollars via exports. The US was largely self-sufficient with a high tariff wall and in fact Europe had little to sell to the US and little it needed, while its own demands for American goods were enormous.

However, apart from preventing the possible collapse of Europe, there were two further policy objectives behind Marshall Aid. The US saw it as a means to restore a world economic system that fitted American ideals of multilateral trade (as opposed to bilateral trade – i.e. balancing trade between two states) and full convertibility of currencies (i.e. buying dollars with pounds or francs freely and without limit). This was the international system that completely broke down in 1929–32 and had not been restored by 1947–48. If currencies were freely convertible again, it would facilitate the buying of goods from anywhere. France, Belgium, the Netherlands and Britain were the centres of currency areas that extended into Asia and Africa (because of their colonial territories). Interconvertibility of these European currencies with each other and ultimately with dollars would automatically lead to a freer world trade and exchange system throughout the non-Soviet world. For the US, Britain and the Sterling Area was the vital component to achieving inter-currency convertibility and multi-lateralism as 50 per cent of the world's trade was conducted with pounds sterling in the late 1940s.

During World War II the UK had created a Sterling Area, a system of strict exchange and import controls and bilateral payments. There were agreements for Imperial and Commonwealth trading preferences (e.g. in 1933 the Australian duty on whiskey was £2.36 per gallon and the preference £0.36). London was the centre for members' sterling balances operating a Sterling Area 'dollar pool' because of the dollar shortages. The UK regarded the Sterling Area as essential to the country's recovery and maintaining sterling's status as a world currency and London as the world's financial centre. The US did not like this as it meant that the UK could buy, using sterling, from those to whom it could sell. The Sterling Area and system of Commonwealth and Imperial preferences meant Britain effectively had its own closed multilateral system. The US Treasury and State Department wanted a multilateral non-discriminatory international economy. From 1941 US and British officials – notably the UK economist John Maynard Keynes and US Harry White – tried to find common ground for a joint post-war policy. However, due to the growing imbalance in their respective powers, Britain had to accept the American plan in the Bretton Woods Agreement. Also, the US only agreed to a $3.75bn loan to Britain in 1945 on condition Britain accepted and agreed to the convertibility of pounds and dollars. This would then mean that 75 per cent of world trade was conducted in convertible currency.

Sterling–dollar convertibility would lead to an international trade and payments system of fixed exchange rates (reversing the 1930s scenario) backed up by the International Monetary Fund (IMF) and GATT. At the core of the Bretton Woods US plan was a *gold backed* dollar as the world's leading currency, with the main institutions – the IMF and the World Bank – located in the US. The clear intention of the US Treasury (and the fear of their UK counterparts) was to shift the locus of economic and financial power to New York away from London.

When convertibility was introduced between sterling and dollars in July 1947, controls had to be reimposed almost immediately in August 1947 (it almost exhausted the $3.75bn credit) as other European states (notably France and Belgium) cashed sterling for dollars and boosted their exports to the UK to earn even more dollars.

The US realised that the sterling crisis and the European dollar shortage were linked. The US Treasury and State Department saw Marshall Aid as a way of fostering European recovery and so fulfilling the Bretton Woods objectives. Milward shows that the 1944 'Bretton Woods system' never had much relevance as a mechanism for European reconstruction – full convertibility was only achieved in 1958 (and the system collapsed in 1971 when the automatic convertibility of dollars to gold ended). Meanwhile, in Western Europe, the European Payments Union was established in 1950 and the ECSC in 1951 (Newton, 1984, pp. 391–3; Milward, 1984, pp. 43–5). It was an illusion that ERP was a step towards the Bretton Woods objectives. The US had hoped that by closing the dollar gap between America and Europe the Bretton Woods principles would become established (Newton, 1984, pp. 401–7; Milward, 1984, p. 476).

The final but by no means least significant American motive for Marshall Aid or the ERP was that it aimed to use the lure of $22bn of aid 1948–52 to try rather overambitiously to achieve the total political reconstruction of Western Europe, and not simply its recovery. Ernest Bevin and Georges Bidault sent invitations for the ERP Conference in July 1947 to Eastern Europe as well as to the 16 Western European countries. Poland asked the USSR whether they could accept and were told to reject it. Czechoslovakia simply accepted. Jan Masaryk (the Czech Foreign Minister) was summoned to see Stalin in Moscow and ordered to withdraw. A few months later in March 1948 the Czechoslovakian government was overthrown by a communist coup and Masaryk was killed (he was thrown out of a window). These tragic events played a large part in stimulating the US Congress to pass Marshall Aid into law as the Economic Co-operation Act of 1948.

The USSR's satellites could have been allowed to accept Marshall Aid and then have disrupted the whole scheme from within. Why did they not try to do this? C.P. Kindleberger, Chief of the US State Department's German-Austrian Economic Affairs Group, thinks it was the Soviet fear of contamination from exposure to western ideas and artefacts (Kindleberger, 1983).

The US wanted to see the economic integration of Western Europe into one common economic regional bloc within the lifespan of the ERP, and ultimately into a common political area. The US aimed to sweep away the nation state system and pressure the 16 OEEC states to integrate into a 'free trade Customs Union'. Such a merger would lead to a 'United States of Europe' including part of Germany (Milward, 1984, p. 467). A cohesive integrated European economic bloc, immune from the economic nationalism and protectionism of the 1930s, would safely accommodate a new West German state and its economic recovery. The US vision of an economically integrated Europe of the 16 OEEC states was a liberal, free-trade, all-embracing common market (rather similar to the vision of Euro-federalists). Enormous pressure was exerted by the US on Britain to take the lead in this integration process, and on France and the other states involved. British officials believed they were being harried constantly by the Americans to bring about European unity. Britain felt that US ideas on Europe were hastily devised and rather ill-conceived. Moreover, given that only 25 per cent of the UK's trade was with Europe, Britain's dollar shortage was dependent on the rest of the world (not Europe) getting dollars. Britain and Europe saw the problem as having insufficient dollars to continue recovery. The US saw the problem as one of insufficient production (Milward, 1982, p. 510).

The CEEC, the large conference of Western European participants in the ERP, met in Paris in the summer of 1947 in response to the offer of Marshall Aid. The US hoped that this would be the first stage in a process of integration as the 16 participant states had to draw up a plan for European recovery acceptable to the US Administration and to the US Congress (which eventually approved it by large majorities in March 1948). The US saw the formation of a Customs Union as central to Europe's ability to co-operate and the willingness of Britain particularly to integrate into Western Europe. However, as Milward points out, the CEEC did not lay the foundations of European co-operation, much less integration; rather, it revealed the disagreements between states and the wide gap between Western European and American views.

The fact that the Conference did not produce the results expected in Washington, with a quick early move to integration, meant 'the heaviest diplomatic pressures were brought to bear on the CEEC' and blame was laid at the door of the British and French (Newton, 1984, p. 395; Milward, 1982, p. 514; 1984, p. 467). Milward shows that French policy towards Germany (pre-summer 1948) was partition, dismemberment and permanent weakening, whereas the UK–US policy was *Bizone* (the economic fusion of the two zones) in order to foster the gradual controlled economic and political revival of a smaller German state. This basic difference meant that little could really be decided about European integration or even economic co-operation inside the CEEC or OEEC. Nothing could be decided on a permanent European framework for reconstruction (such as the form of a Customs Union), as far as France was concerned until the 'German question' had been answered.

Determined pressure from the US led to the UK suggesting the formation of the CUSG in 1947 through the CEEC. This met in Brussels rather than Paris, away from American interference, and was an attempt by Britain, France *et al.* to explore possible European designs for a smaller West European Customs Union. It was through this route of CUSG discussions that the shape and form of the first European Community eventually emerged in the Franco-German association of the Schuman Plan. As Milward shows, the CUSG was a much more significant step towards the formation of the European Community than the CEEC, OEEC or EPU.

Such was the diplomatic pressure on Britain in 1948 from the US that the Departmental Under-Secretary of State, Roger Makins, noted in July 1948 that the UK's 'inability to find policies sufficiently spectacular to influence Congress' might mean the UK having to 'take a plunge' and 'rash action in the last resort' of setting up a Customs Union. Other Foreign Office officials considered establishing 'a sham Customs Union' as a sop to American pressure (Boyle, 1982, p. 382).

The CEEC was superseded eventually by the OEEC a year later in 1948 – a standing conference that eventually developed into a bureaucracy of 1,000 people. The US policy was to try to mould the OEEC Council as a prototype Western European Federal Government and a first step to building a United States of Europe. Part of the US strategy was to make the OEEC itself allocate ERP funds. However, although the OEEC was supposed to divide up US aid and so in the process foster an integrated European organisation, according to Milward it only ever produced a 'scramble for dollars' by the member states and was never a real forum for European co-operation, let alone integration (16 countries' interests and views were too diverse).

In 1949 the US wanted the OEEC to have a Director-General with real executive supranational powers (referred to as 'Superman' in UK Foreign Office documents!). The US conspired with Belgium to get Paul-Henri Spaak, the ex-Prime Minister, into this post (who was out of office by August 1949). Although it was Britain that vetoed this move – to the fury of the Americans – the Scandinavians, Dutch and French were just as opposed.

Following this the US abandoned both the attempts to get the OEEC to allocate and distribute ERP funds and any hope that the policy machinery of the OEEC could somehow be transformed via constitutional change into an integrated supranational political organisation for Western Europe (Milward, 1984, p. 206).

The US also finally saw that the UK could not be forced into European integration. However the US did not abandon its central goal of European integration. It simply pursued a different track towards a European Customs Union by creating a single large market through trade liberalisation in Europe and the abolition of administrative and legal protective barriers to trade between West European states (where tariffs, quotas, quantity restrictions proliferated). Paul Hoffman, the US Administrator of the Marshall Aid Programme, elaborated this in Autumn 1949: 'the substance of such integration would be the formation of a large single market within which quantitative restrictions on the movements of goods, monetary barriers to the flow of payments and, eventually, all tariffs are permanently swept away'.

To sweep away monetary barriers to the flow of payments and foster the US Bretton Woods objective of one trade and payments system for the western (non-Soviet) world the US promoted the European Payments Union (EPU) Treaty. This was signed on 19 September 1950 (the negotiations were only concluded after the outbreak of the Korean War). The EPU aid did much to encourage and facilitate intra-European trade from 1950 and was the first European organisation which incorporated the FRG. The Americans again hoped that the EPU machinery would provide a functional basis for European integration and lead to monetary union in Europe. In this they were to be disappointed. The US was insistent on full convertibility but the UK's priority was to defend sterling against the threat of convertibility. Britain was not keen on the automatic clearing of all multilateral settlements in Europe (when pound–dollar convertibility was tried three years before in July 1947, Belgium's conversion of sterling balances into dollars had caused a run on the pound). The US therefore had to settle in the EPU for a more limited form of multilateralism, having to continue dollar aid to make this possible and face continued discrimination against US goods through the 1950s in Western Europe (Milward, 1984, pp. 326, 333).

The UK was in a strong bargaining position for two reasons. Britain could always threaten to withdraw into the Sterling Area (the 'siege economy' option). This was effectively Britain's own 'multilateral' Imperial trade system based on the pound. Inside dollars were unnecessary. However, this would have divided the world into two payments systems (US hard, UK soft), i.e. the very opposite of the American idea behind the Bretton Woods 'one world' approach. Also, the 1949 sterling crisis and devaluation saw the UK dollar reserves drop to danger level again and made the UK *more* resistant to the US policy. The US had to give way to the UK inside the EPU.

American Marshall Aid was important for maintaining capital goods imports into Europe, so sustaining European economic recovery by a high rate of capital formation in the late 1940s. Between 1946–53 West Germany got $3.6bn, most of it before the end of 1950. What Marshall Aid did, according to Kindleberger, was to restock warehouse shelves and the component bins of factories. Inventories were well below minimum levels in Germany in 1947 in everything except scrap metal (Kindleberger, 1987, pp. 194–6). Marshall Aid 'restocked all Europe', although Kindleberger thinks the effect of Marshall Aid on the economic recovery was exaggerated by the severe winter of 1947 and good harvest of 1948 (Kindleberger, 1987, pp. 102–3).

The ERP had less success with its other connected objectives of facilitating the US vision for a Bretton Woods system, which was a multilateral trading world with fixed exchange rates and full currency convertibility, and a United States of Europe with 16 states creating a federation with a free-trade, liberal Customs Union at its core. Indeed, as Milward has shown, it was doubtful whether these were compatible objectives, i.e. whether the ERP could have been a step towards a return to Bretton Woods. From 1949 the American administration of ERP and the whole programme was actually under attack in Washington for impeding the solution to a world trade and payments system (Milward, 1984, p. 476).

The combination of $22bn in aid and relentless diplomatic pressure from the US was not enough to impose their own framework for European reconstruction. Why were the Americans unsuccessful in imposing their solution and how were they thwarted? While the EPU in 1950 and the ECSC in 1950–51 were the result of US pressure for integration, to a greater extent they reflected the national interests and wishes of Britain and France. These two states, although unable to ignore US pressure, were capable of blocking American designs for Western Europe to integrate through the OEEC framework even when the US had successfully allied itself with small countries (like Belgium – often seen in London as the tool of US policy in Europe). American policy from 1947 was to create a large all-embracing free-trade common market in Europe. Why did France oppose this?

In the first place it could not satisfy the first requirement of French foreign policy – a solution to the German question. French policy towards Germany until the summer of 1948 was to see it permanently weakened and dismembered, with the Ruhr made an autonomous zone under international control with its resources available for French and Benelux exploitation. French insistence on this led ultimately to the compromise of an International Ruhr Authority being established in 1948. Anglo-American policy on the other hand was to merge their two German zones economically (*Bizonia*) and gradually revive the German economy. This difference in policy and the fact that no firm decisions had been taken towards the future Germany by the four occupying powers (UK, US, USSR, France) meant that there was no prospect of France agreeing to join any Customs Union without an answer to the German question. Two events compelled France to rethink. The first was currency reform in the Western Zones on 20 June 1948 based on the recommendations of the Colm–Dodge–Goldsmith Report of a 10:1 conversion of Reichmarks to Deutschmarks. This shrank the money supply to a point where they were able to abandon price control, restore the incentive to work, buy goods in the open market and end hoarding and the black market (Kindleberger,

1987, p. 102). The other was the London Conference of July 1948 where the process of reconstructing a West German state commenced.

France then started seriously to envisage a new Franco-German economic association and to explore within the CUSG the possibility of a 'Little Europe' Customs Union, not the 'Big Europe' of 16 states that the US preferred.

The second reason for the lack of US success was that even after this shift in French policy towards Germany the American conception of a Western Europe Customs Union as 'Big Europe' was at variance with the French concept of a 'Little Europe' that was evolving in 1948–50 as a small, closely regulated common market. The French knew that despite the 1946 Monnet Plan their economy was not yet sufficiently competitive and their economic recovery would suffer in a big, liberal free-trade Customs Union. In the French-style dirigiste Common Market there was an attempt to anticipate the consequences and, through negotiation, to control and distribute gains and losses in advance, i.e. actually direct and apportion the economic consequences of a common market before it came into effect. If accurate this process should safeguard members' national interests and so 'guarantee' the success of the Customs Union by ensuring 'fair' trade rather than purely 'free' trade. This was far from the US conception of a liberal free-trade Customs Union, which for the French represented far too great a gamble. France's Schuman Plan of 1950, however, appeared to be a solution both to the German question and for ensuring French modernisation and economic recovery within an integrated organisation.

In the case of EPU, the US was forced to accede to British vested interests and requirements and in the ECSC to those of France (Milward, 1984, p. 333). This was perhaps inescapable as the US had little alternative for reaching their dream or implementing their vision other than by persuading West Europeans to adopt it for themselves. (The USSR in contrast imposed their political and economic vision of central planning and a command economy on Eastern Europe.) European integration in 1947 was considered impossible without France and Britain; in 1949 it was still inconceivable without France. By then the UK had reverted to 'limited liability', turning its back economically on Europe and focusing on the Sterling Area and Commonwealth. This was ironic given US policy on Europe and the importance of the special relationship to Britain. France then had the chance to create a French-style Little Europe to suit her interests, which in 1948–49 became a more urgent matter with the gradual emergence of a reconstituted West German state.

Nevertheless by 1950, as Milward's meticulous painstaking research demonstrates, the twin pillars of the EPU and ECSC were the start of a reconstructed framework for Western Europe – the new architecture successfully incorporated the newborn West German state with a booming economy (Milward, 1984, p. 367, Table 51; its steel output was 2.72m tonnes 1946, 11.93m tonnes 1950). In this the US was entitled to take much credit because, as Kindleberger argues, without Marshall Aid it would have taken West Germany a long time to refill its empty raw material bins (Kindleberger, 1987, p. 261). The US also encouraged European integration with a clumsy yet vigorous persistence through any available channel and brought a West German state into existence, as a by-product of its Cold War rivalry with the USSR, 1948–49.

The route to the Schuman Plan of 1950 leading to the ECSC in 1951 can be traced back to the advent of Marshall Aid and the CEEC in Paris, July 1947. Britain's CEEC delegation suggested setting up the CUSG in September 1947 based in Brussels. It was within this body's discussions that many ideas embodied in the Schuman Plan were incubating between 1948–50.

When some selected German politicians from the Bizone were first told, in October 1948, of the possibility of creating a Customs Union incorporating West Germany they were 'barely restrained from making an immediate demand for the adoption of a Customs Union at once' (Milward, 1984, p. 250). Such was their desperation to embark on the political rehabilitation of their new country's old reputation with its neighbours.

# Part II

# Development

# Chapter 4

# The Schuman Plan (1950) and the European Coal and Steel Community (1951)

On 9 May 1950 Robert Schuman, the French Foreign Minister 1948–52, made his surprise announcement proposing the pooling of coal and steel production. Following protracted negotiations, the Treaty of Paris was signed by 'the Six' on 19 March 1951, which established the supranational ECSC. This created a common market for coal, steel, coke, iron ore and scrap between France, Germany, Belgium, the Netherlands, Luxembourg and Italy. Britain declined to participate in the talks from the outset.

The fact that coal and steel were the first economic sectors to be incorporated into an integrated organisation is acknowledgement of their central importance to nation states' economic and military power. Coal and steel had provided both the military capacity for invasion as well as being a motive for German and French territorial acquisition. Alsace-Lorraine, a French province, and its iron ore deposits changed hands between France and Germany in 1871, 1918, 1940 and 1945. The Saar, a German district rich in coal, was administered by the League of Nations, 1919–35, with its mines controlled by the French to compensate for German damage to French coalmines in the World War I. Following World War II the French again ran the Saarland for its coal between 1945–57. (Plebiscites in 1935 and 1957 resulted in Saarlanders opting to rejoin Germany.) Robert Schuman himself came from the disputed territory of Alsace. He fought in the German army in 1914–18, had German as his first language and only became a French citizen in 1919.

Germany had big reserves of coking coal (used in steel production), whereas France, not being well endowed geologically with coal, depended on German coal supplies. Geology, economics and foreign policy became inevitably and tragically intertwined – it was a significant component of Franco-German relations and rivalry. In January 1923 French and Belgian troops had occupied the coal-producing Ruhr Basin as Germany failed to pay its quota of war reparations (under the terms of the Treaty of

Versailles 1919). There was a precedent here as, following defeat in the Franco-Prussian War 1870, France had to pay a five billion franc indemnity in 1871 to Germany whose army remained in France until it was paid. During World War II, under German occupation 75 per cent of French iron ore production and 15 per cent of French coal output was compulsorily exported to Germany. In 1944 this traffic accounted for 85 per cent of all rail movements in France.

At the end of the war in 1945 it was assumed by West European states, occupied by Germany between 1940–44, that their access to German coal and markets would be safeguarded and German steel output heavily restricted. Steel was the major element in states' post-war economic reconstruction (needed for railways, buildings, ships, vehicles, machinery). After the war, Norway and the Netherlands started their own steel industries for the first time. The demand for steel was high and there was a shortage of raw material inputs.

After the war German steel production was restricted by the Allied Coal and Steel Control Boards and military governments – whereas in 1938 German steel output amounted to 38 per cent of Europe's total, by 1949 it was 18 per cent (Milward, 1984, p. 371). The Petersburg Protocols imposed limits on German shipyard capacity, ship size and speed (controls which lasted until 1952) and German steel plants came under the statutory authority of US and UK military governments. The production limit for steel was 7.5m tonnes in 1946. Dismantling of many listed German steel works – Herman Goering works at Salzgitter, Krupps at Essen and Thyssens at Hambourn – continued in French and British zones until 1949. German coal and steel industries were both 'decartelised' (the six biggest steel companies were broken into 24 smaller ones) and 'deconcentrated' – in 1944 33 per cent of coal production in Germany was controlled by steel companies, by 1947 it was 16 per cent (Milward, 1984, pp. 369, 371, 384–6, 411).

In France the Monnet Plan for the Modernization and Re-equipment of the French Economy that started in March 1946 was intended eventually to make the French economy internationally competitive and, following the 'lesson of 1940', to reverse the technological inferiority of the French economy. In 1946 France had 0.5 million machine tools, many of which were 20 years old, whereas Germany had 1.5 million, which were more modern. The success of the Monnet Plan, intended to rectify such relative technological weakness, depended on three conditions being met. The first, according to Frances Lynch, was France getting priority access to the Ruhr's resources of coal and coke – that is, priority over Germany for the Ruhr's coal. The second was that French industry must recover and reconstruct before Germany's economy revived, as German industry had lower production costs (16 per cent lower in the case of steel making). Finally, the Monnet Plan aimed to replace German goods in both Germany and her export markets with French goods (Lynch, 1984, pp. 233, 235, 239).

Therefore, as Lynch shows, the Monnet Plan for the modernisation of the French economy was originally based on 'the traditional view that French political and economic strength lay in German weakness' (Lynch, 1984, p. 242). The best guarantee of French security, peace and avoiding a fourth German invasion was not the reassurance of the protection of France by her allies via guarantees in treaties, but by limiting German capacity for steel production and expanding French steel and heavy industry through access both to German coking coal resources and German markets. French foreign policy towards Germany clearly reflected these French national economic interests enshrined in the Monnet Plan – the permanent dismemberment of the German state, the Ruhr being made an International Zone separate from Germany; and the dismantling, deconcentration and decartelisation of the German steel industry.

The problem for France was that this policy proved unacceptable to the Americans and British: it would mean that the US would have to pay continually to keep German steel-making capacity under-utilised and German labour idle to the detriment of the European Recovery Programme as a whole. While it was US policy in 1945 to limit expenditure on Germany (under directive JCS1067) to the avoidance of 'disease and unrest', this formula was abandoned with the Cold War and Marshall Aid. The Western Zones of Germany received $3.6bn in 1947–50, which along with monetary reform and the Berlin blockade (the coal and steel kept out of West Berlin ironically helped West Germany's revival) fuelled economic expansion. Steel production doubled in a year and coal output rose by 50 per cent, and by 1949 industrial output was at 80 per cent of the 1936 level (Kindleberger, 1987, pp. 34–5, 196). German steel production, which had been 'fixed' at the limit of 7.5m tonnes in 1946, was fixed again at 11m in 1947 by the Allied Control Commission, much to the annoyance of Georges Bidault, the French Foreign Minister 1947–48, who argued that with sufficient German coking coal France and the Benelux could produce any increased output.

By the summer of 1948 at the London Conference France had to accommodate herself to two approaching unpalatable developments – the gradual emergence of a new West German State and the revival of its economy. Much of the Conference was devoted to the issue of the exact remit of the International Authority for the Ruhr, which had been set up to placate France, over future allocations of German coking coal and steel production controls. Although the International Authority of the Ruhr from 28 December 1948 divided quantities of Ruhr coke, coal and steel between domestic and export markets with a compulsory allocation to France in accordance with the OEEC programme, in reality it had little real power and no control over German coal and steel production, which remained with UK and US military governments' Coal and Steel Control Boards. It was another rather weak interdependent organisation lacking power and any guarantee of permanence (Milward, 1984, pp. 157, 160). Achieving the conditions required for the Monnet Plan's success looked more remote with this prospect of a revived German state and economy.

This setback to the issue of overriding importance in French foreign policy was potentially dangerous, requiring an urgent solution. It threatened both national security and French national economic recovery through the Monnet Plan. If France opposed the emergence of a West German state, the British and Americans could go ahead anyway in their Bizone and France would appear as an adversary of German democratic revival: undermining French influence over West Germany as a whole and jeopardising any prospect of Franco-German association or co-operation.

French planners had to find a way to guarantee the future of its modernisation and in effect the Schuman Plan subsequently rescued the Monnet Plan, as it guaranteed continued French access to the resources of the Ruhr (Milward, 1984, p. 475; Lynch, 1984, p. 242). The issue of a Customs Union including West Germany was examined in the CUSG from 1948. German economic recovery meant a rising tide of exports from Western Europe to Germany in 1949, cut off from its Eastern sources of grain and potatoes (Kindleberger, 1987, p. 39), revealing both the need for and possible advantages of a common market to France and the Netherlands.

Following the 1948 London Conference, Robert Schuman recognised the urgent need for a radical change in French policy towards Germany. The only alternative (to their 1944-48 policy of weakening and dismembering Germany) was a more positive policy of co-operation or association. Dean Acheson, US Secretary of State 1949-53, recognised that only France could integrate Europe (by 1949 it was clear that Britain would not) and he made a personal appeal to Schuman to take the initiative to reconcile West Germany to Western Europe (Milward, 1984, pp. 391-2).

Jean Monnet, who was head of the planning organisation – he was

Commissariat Général au Plan and eventually High Commissioner of the modernisation and re-equipment plan – played a formative role in the Schuman Plan and invented the concept of a supranational body – the 'High Authority' to run the ECSC. Monnet, who was neither an elected politician nor a French professional civil servant, led the French negotiations with West Germany and the other four states in 1950–51. Jean Monnet subsequently became the first President of the High Authority of the ECSC. Whether he was, as he is invariably seen in retrospect, 'the founding father of Europe', Monnet certainly rescued the modernisation and re-equipment plan and so safeguarded French national economic interests and preserved security, through starting a Franco-German alliance, which has now endured for more than 40 years.

Frances Lynch (1984, p. 242) argues that to disguise the highly political nature of the Schuman Plan the ECSC was created under a smokescreen of idealistic European rhetoric. Statements by Schuman that it was 'the first concrete foundation of European federation' were music to American ears and satisfied the US Congress that Marshall Aid was creating a European framework to contain Germany. Dissimulation concealed this second French attempt to reshape Europe's economic and political environment to suit the needs of the French domestic economy, safeguarding French reconstruction plans by creating a common market in coal and steel, so providing equal access for France to the Ruhr's resources.

What did the ECSC actually do? Schuman's original announcement on 9 May 1950 proposed that 'the entire French and German production of coal and steel be placed under a joint High Authority within an organization open to the participation of other European nations'. The High Authority was to ensure the supply of coal on equal terms inside a common market. France was keen to end the dual-pricing of coal (with German domestic coal prices lower than for exported coal) and discriminatory freight rates that in 1950 made the price of German coke in Lorraine, France, 46 per cent higher than the Ruhr (Milward, 1984, pp. 378–9), giving German steelmakers a significant cost advantage over France.

The Treaty of Paris 1951 was a complex commercial treaty establishing the ECSC as a regulated market-sharing arrangement under supranational control. It was designed to balance the six states' particular vested interests in coal and steel and to facilitate achievement of national objectives in these two sectors. The common external tariff of the ECSC's Customs Union was fixed lower than that of France but higher than the

Benelux and a five-year transition period was allowed before full operation of the agreement.

Italy was allowed nevertheless to retain its full tariff to protect its small, high-cost steel industry within the Common Market. Scrap was included in the agreement as this constituted the prime raw material for Italian electric-arc process steel making. Italy also got access to French North African iron ore resources (Milward, 1984, p. 414).

There were complicated arrangements for fixing the price of coal. Prices were set artificially high to allow the restructuring costs of Belgium's declining coal industry to be subsidised mainly from the Netherlands and Germany by $45m between 1953–58 with another $5m as an export subsidy for Belgian coal (Milward, 1984, p. 399; 1992, chapter 3).

France negotiating from a strong bargaining position 1949–51 obtained equal access to the Ruhr's resources within the Common Market and the end of dual-pricing and discriminatory freight rates. France had received $205m for coking plant from the High Authority's investment funds by 1958. In 1952 German steel prices were increased to virtually close the gap between French and German prices prior to the common market in steel coming into operation. Germany also agreed that France would supply the Southern German market with steel for three years (243,000 tonnes in 1952 and 855,000 tonnes in 1954). German car exports from South Germany were manufactured from the output of modern French strip-rolling steel mills (constructed under the Monnet Plan) in the Thionville and Metz area (Milward, 1984, pp. 413–14). Overall German imports of steel doubled between 1953–56 because of the booming German economy and the ECSC agreement.

The ECSC created a single common market from six national markets, in coal, steel, coke and scrap metal, but also safeguarded specific national interests, as in Italy's case, assisted Belgium grappling with its ailing coal sector and facilitated, through international agreement, French national economic objectives. The essential elements of the Monnet Plan were indeed rescued by the Schuman Plan, as Lynch and Milward's research demonstrates, the ECSC providing equal access to Ruhr coal and guaranteed markets for French steel in Germany. Moreover, the supranational High Authority meant the collective day-to-day control and regulation of steel and coal markets throughout the Common Market and therefore within West Germany itself. How else might France and Benelux, in the circumstances of 1948–50, have exercised real, certain, durable or better influence over West Germany's coal and steel sectors?

For Monnet, Schuman and Quai d'Orsay officials of the French Foreign Ministry the solution by 1949 of a Franco-German association in an integrated organisation under supranational control was inspired by France's two bad post-war experiences in the 1920s (starting with the failure of the Treaty of Versailles 1919 and the 1927 Treaty) and in 1946– 47 (with the Allied Control Council's 'fixed limits' on German steel output being raised regularly). The French were understandably extremely sceptical of the value of treaty guarantees that relied for compliance only on the good faith and consistency of national governments. (France had also broken a 'solemn obligation' contracted with Britain in June 1940 by concluding a separate peace with Germany.) The Treaty of Paris 1951, in contrast, created the first integrated organisation offering the prospects of permanent compliance – with a supranational High Authority policing the Treaty and a Court of Justice to settle disputes. This was Monnet's ingenious solution to the problem of co-existing and conducting business securely with Germany. The bold brave political act of Schuman – a massive 'U-turn' in French policy to Germany – created a Franco- German alliance that has endured for 45 years and laid the basis for peace and prosperity in Western Europe since 1950.

Why did West Germany agree to join this alliance on basically French terms? What did West Germany hope to gain from the Treaty of Paris 1951? When the Federal Republic emerged in May 1949 made up of the UK, US and French zones, it was still subject to numerous restrictions and controls. The Occupation Statute prohibited full responsibility for foreign affairs, defence or foreign trade, and ownership and decartelisation of Ruhr industries. The International Authority of the Ruhr 1948 undertook the compulsory allocation of coal between domestic and export markets. Konrad Adenauer, Federal Chancellor 1949–63, had as his main objective the removal of these irksome constraints and to obtain full sovereignty for his fledgling state (in fact West Germany could only start negotiations over the ECSC with the permission of the Allied High Commission in the Federal Republic). Adenauer's strategy for achieving this was full co-operation and close collaboration with the three western powers. For Adenauer, therefore, political considerations were of upmost importance in negotiating the Treaty of Paris 1951. Adenauer was keen to co-operate with France on equal terms and he insisted on equal terms of entry for the FRG into the ECSC.

In the negotiations France was helped by US pressure on the FRG to accept French terms and by using the International Authority of the Ruhr as a bargaining counter. Professor Walter Hallstein, State Secretary in the Office of the Federal Chancellor 1950, negotiating for the FRG, was told by Monnet that if West Germany accepted the Schuman Plan France would press for the abolition of the International Authority for the Ruhr.

Indeed when the Treaty of Paris was signed in April 1951 controls on the German steel industry were 'drastically changed' (Milward, 1984, pp. 412, 420), with the end of most of the economic constraints imposed after the Potsdam Conference in 1945.

So the FRG made political gains from the Treaty of Paris by winning recognition as an equal partner having equal status and by the removal of most of the limitations and controls over steel and coal. Whereas for France the prime motive for the ECSC was economic (Monnet and the planners prepared the plan which Schuman and the Ministry of Foreign Affairs then took up), for Germany the motives were political. Accepting the Schuman Plan and signing the Treaty of Paris was the only way to commence their national rehabilitation as an independent sovereign state.

For Adenauer too the stated federalist objective underpinning the scheme (regardless of whether motivated by idealism or dissimilation) was politically useful. He wanted Germans to avoid what he called 'bad thoughts' and come to think of themselves as Europeans.

Although initially much of the German and French steel industry was opposed to a common market and Belgium's coal industry was hostile (Milward, 1984, p. 419), experience soon proved it to be very much in their economic interests.

There was opposition from the SPD in Germany which suspected that the ECSC was not an idealistic internationalist plan but a Catholic, conservative and capitalist plot. (Schuman, Adenauer and de Gasperi, Italy's Prime Minister, were Roman Catholics and Christian Democrats, and had German as their first language.) However, Hans Boekler, President of the DGB and German trade unions generally, did not share the SPD's view. In France, Guy Mollet and the SFIO had reservations: they were disappointed at the British Labour government's absence and considered that Monnet and the French government were wrong to require Britain's prior acceptance of a common High Authority before the talks began. Like the SDP, the SFIO suspected a Catholic plot to keep Protestants out. But Monnet had close links with French trade union leaders and kept them well-informed, ensuring that they were represented on the national delegation and dispelling such fears.

Why did Britain not join the scheme? Britain excluded herself from the talks leading to the ECSC as they were unwilling to sign, prior to the start of negotiations, a communiqué with the other governments agreeing in advance to the 'pooling of coal and steel production' and accepting the transfer of national control to a High Authority. For Schuman and Monnet the supranational aspect was vital to French national interests and so non-negotiable. They feared that the UK would work to under-mine this essential element of the Plan if it was open for discussion. So Schuman and Monnet made Britain an offer they were sure would be refused. In fact it would have been surprising if the UK had accepted French terms to join the talks as in January 1949 an interdepartmental meeting of the Foreign Office, Board of Trade and Treasury had decided to revert to 'limited liability' with Europe and prioritise the UK's relations with the US and Commonwealth, relegating European links to secondary status.

The Labour government had nationalised coal in 1946 and the National Coal Board's long-term plan was only published in 1950. Neither the government nor the NCB were prepared to relinquish control to a supranational High Authority eventually based in Luxembourg. Herbert Morrison, Acting Prime Minister, is supposed to have said in the Cabinet discussion: 'It's no good, we cannot do it, the Durham miners won't wear it.' Britain's rather condescending, aloof, introverted response towards the Schuman Plan had much to do with the fact that UK production far out-stripped Western Europe's. In iron and steel, which the government was preparing to nationalise in 1949–50, UK crude steel output (16m tonnes) was approximately half that of the whole of Western Europe. Europe took only 25 per cent of UK trade, the Sterling Area took 50 per cent. Only 5 per cent of UK steel exports went to Europe. The instinctive reaction of cautious British officials to the Schuman Plan was not to take any risks with Britain's steel exports. Why complicate current arrangements by joining the scheme? Moreover, unlike France, Britain relied on her Commonwealth and US connections for access to scarce resources and raw materials. The Foreign Office paid much attention to negotiations for more US steel by arranging to 'swap' aluminium and nickel 'loaned' from Canada and minerals from Rhodesia for American steel.

Even so, some officials like Edwin Plowden, Chairman of the Economic Planning Board 1947–53, thought there might be economic advantages in it for Britain and Sir Stafford Cripps, Chancellor of the Exchequer 1947–50, also thought that the UK should join but fell ill and could not argue his case. The Foreign Office opposed the plan. Ernest Bevin was enraged when he first heard of Schuman's announcement in early May 1950, because of the lack of consultation, advance warning and the preconditions attached. On 1 June 1950 the French government gave Britain a 24-hour ultimatum to accept the terms or the talks would proceed without them. Interestingly, when the talks started, without Britain, the objective had altered. Instead of referring to 'pooling' coal and

LEEDS COLLEGE OF BUILDING LIBRARY
NORTH STREET
LEEDS LS2 7QT
Tel. (0113) 222 6097 and 6098

steel production' as in the 9 May 1950 announcement, the French working paper on the scheme of 27 June 1950 emphasised the High Authority's role as

> to contribute to a policy of economic expansion, of full employment, and of a rising standard of living for the workers . . . it should ensure that the needs of the member countries would be satisfied and exports would be developed without discrimination. This would be achieved under the best possible economic conditions through the establishment of a broad single market.

This appeared both more moderate and attractive as a communal objective. Nevertheless, the Foreign Office viewed the Schuman process not simply as economic integration but as a move towards the political federation of Europe – Schuman had referred to the 'starting point for a United Europe'. The Foreign Office wanted to discourage any emergent supranational European federation – fearing the possibility of it becoming either a neutralist third-force between the two superpowers (Young, 1988, ch. 4, p. 109) or creating a Franco-German superstate. The Foreign Office also thought it unlikely that the continentals would agree among themselves – particularly in the absence of British diplomacy. In fact arguably it proved easier without Britain, as it meant one less bargain to strike during the technical negotiations.

In July 1950 Schuman proposed the 'association' idea to Britain as a way of connecting the UK to the ECSC short of full membership. Subsequently Bevin, Morrison and then Eden after 1951 pursued the same policy of 'close association short of full membership' with both the ECSC and the Pleven Plan's EDC. Eden's Plan was to use the existing Council of Europe's institutions for the ECSC and the EDC. However, Bonn and Rome in particular suspected that Britain wanted to act as a brake on the process of integration. Monnet, too, was fearful of British sabotage. Young shows that as a result by September 1952 the Eden Plan was dead. Eden and the UK then adopted a benevolent attitude towards the ECSC (Young, 1988, ch. 4, pp. 110, 113–15, 118) and proceeded to formulate the terms of the UK's association. Paradoxically, an internal Foreign Office 'Schuman Plan Committee' report proposed in 1953 that the UK should actually join a common market in steel as the competition would be good for the industry and also recognised that the 'Schuman Community could create a unit of great economic power with which the UK must come to terms'. Peter Thorneycroft, President of the Board of Trade, was also willing to consider UK entry into a common market for steel. The Commonwealth, when consulted on their reaction to a closer

UK–ECSC link, did not object at all. Canada and New Zealand supported it and Australia and South Africa accepted British assurances that Commonwealth interests would be safeguarded (Young, 1988, ch. 4, pp. 123–4). The real opposition came from the steel, coal and engineering industries and trade unions in 1953–54 and also from the Treasury. Rab Butler, Chancellor of the Exchequer 1951–55, was very hostile to the idea of closer links with the ECSC. Eden also did not want to do anything to encourage European integration (which ruled out joining a common market) yet at the same time had to avoid appearing to sabotage the process (which would have enraged the Americans). This only left a rather limited form of 'association' as a policy option.

Moreover, if in 1953–54 the UK had decided to join a common market in steel, in spite of opposition from industry and elsewhere, it would have been much harder to argue the case for Britain keeping out of the EDC. A closer UK–ECSC link would have encouraged 'the Six' and the Americans to increase the pressure on Britain to join the scheme for a European army. The UK's long delayed association agreement with the ECSC was only finalised in December 1954 after the EDC scheme had been dead and buried for four months.

1954 was the third but not the last missed opportunity by Britain to join an integrated Europe. In retrospect this policy choice can be seen as a costly failure as the Common Market proved to be a more successful commercial venture than the UK's Commonwealth links.

However, unlike France in 1950, the UK's vested economic interests and national recovery were not dependent on commercial links with Germany and, unlike France, the UK did not see the main threat to its national security as a resurgent West Germany. The French-integrated solution of a Franco-German association under a supranational High Authority when presented as the first move towards a United Europe was guaranteed to appeal to Americans and repel the British.

How did the ECSC operate? The parliaments of the six states surrendered sovereignty over coal and steel to the supranational High Authority which assumed full executive power over these sectors. The Authority consisted of nine members in office for six years; eight were designated by the governments of 'the Six' acting together and the ninth was elected by the original eight members. The High Authority members, president, and auditor of accounts, were appointed jointly by the participant governments – none of them were simply nominees of individual states.

Negotiations between July 1950 and March 1951 reduced the derogation of national sovereignty involved. At the insistence of the

Netherlands and Belgium, a Council of Ministers modified the powers of the High Authority. The High Authority could issue 'decisions' which were binding, 'recommendations' which were binding in objective but not in the means to obtain them, and 'opinions' which had no binding force. The High Authority was assisted by a rather ineffectual consultative committee of between 30 and 51 producers, workers, consumers and dealers. On certain specific issues the High Authority was obliged to consult this committee but was free to ignore its advice. The High Authority was responsible to a Parliamentary Assembly, which at its short annual session to consider the Authority's report, could cause the Authority to resign en masse by passing a vote of censure by a two-thirds majority. As Schuman said:

> for the first time, an international assembly would be more than a consultative organ; the parliaments themselves, having surrendered a fraction of their sovereignty, would regain that sovereignty, through its common exercise.

A Court of Justice was established to settle national disputes and hear industrial appeals.

In August 1952, after ratification by the six parliaments, the ECSC started to function and in 1953 the Common Market commenced operations. Between 1952–62 iron ore production increased from 62m to 92m tonnes, new patterns of trade developed and there was a greater harmonisation of working conditions. Early opposition to the scheme by industrialists, most notably in France but also in Belgium and the Ruhr, soon dissipated as did exaggerated fears of the competitive strength of other producers. The ECSC operated successfully for 20 years apart from technical difficulties and a crisis in 1958 when coal surpluses, unsold stocks and cheap US coal caused problems. The High Authority proposed to fix production quotas but governments rejected this idea and started to take unilateral action to safeguard their own coal and steel interests.

This 1958 crisis in the ECSC coincided with the start of the EEC and Euratom that marked a decline in political influence of the ECSC, whose institutions were eventually absorbed by these new communities in 1967. However, overall, the ECSC successfully functioned through the 1950s and 1960s when demand and production were expanding, guaranteeing equal French access both to Ruhr coal and German markets.

The political impact of the ECSC was also significant. The institutions operated well and rules on competition were agreed easily, to the surprise and relief of the nine-man High Authority. Europeans from states which had spent years at war with each other proved quite capable of working and co-operating together, obeying common rules and paying a common tax. A group of influential ministers, civil servants, journalists, trade unionists and industrialists from the six states worked together on a daily basis. Monnet, as first President of the ECSC, formed a tight cohesive cadre of enthusiastic evangelical 'Eurocrats' at the Luxembourg head-quarters. The Parliamentary Assembly served almost as a graduate school for European integration to many of the leading politicians of 'the Six' – people like Erich Ollenhauer, who succeeded Schumacher after his death in 1952, as leader of the SPD in West Germany. Such developments were to have an effect on future initiatives in 'Little Europe' after 1954.

Meanwhile, in June 1950, only four weeks after Schuman announced his plan, the Korean War started. Events in the Far East were to affect the whole process of European integration over the next four years.

# Chapter 5

# German rearmament, the European Defence Community and the demise of the European army, 1950–54

The European Defence Community never came into existence, so why bother to consider it? There are two reasons for doing so. The EDC and the ECSC plans were in fact closely linked. The team that drafted the ECSC scheme also devised the EDC. In the summer of 1950 the prospect of German rearmament in NATO offered an alternative route than the ECSC for Germany to regain full control over its industry. The EDC was intended to stop this and so protect the ECSC until signed and in force.

The EDC scheme of civil and military integration was contrived to protect economic integration in the ECSC, a device for delaying West Germany's rearmament and its complete control of national and foreign affairs.

The issue of rearming the West Germans first arose in 1949 when the USSR exploded its first atomic device. This was much sooner than the US expected, and was partly as a result of Soviet spies at the Los Alamos research laboratories and KGB scientists interviewing the theoretical physicist Niels Bohr in Denmark after the war. Some consideration was given then, by the US, to the question of West German rearmament and strengthening ground defence. There was, however, no urgency despite Soviet conventional military superiority – the Russians had 22 divisions out of 175 in Eastern Europe as a whole, compared with two each for the US and UK in West Germany out of a total of 14 NATO divisions (Kirby, 1977, p. 100; Dockrill, 1991, p. 10). The American nuclear umbrella over Europe was still a credible deterrent – the US had an effective monopoly of atomic weapons, as the USSR had no delivery system until 1955, when a long-range Tupolev bomber came into service. The US was also developing 'the super' fusion H-bomb from 1950, testing a device in 1952 and the weapon in 1954. Yet it was clearly recognised that once US nuclear superiority started to fade in the mid-to-late 1950s, so the deterrent effect of American nuclear retaliation to a Soviet invasion of Western Europe would also decline. Then the US would be keen to improve conventional forces, including a West German contribution by the late 1950s.

West German rearmament only became an issue in 1950 because of the Korean War. This war made German rearmament a predominant theme of US policy in Western Europe. On 25 June 1950 the North Korean army equipped with Russian-built tanks and supported by Soviet Yak fighters crossed the 38th Parallel into South Korea, sweeping aside lightly armed South Korean troops. News of this Soviet-backed communist invasion of South Korea caused a wave of panic in West Berlin and Dr Konrad Adenauer wanted immediate reinforcements to be sent (Dockrill, 1991, p. 22). Why? What relevance did Korea have? The fear was that the Elbe could become another '38th Parallel', the worst possible scenario being a Soviet–East German invasion of West Germany. Although, unlike South Korea, the presence of American, British and French forces in West Berlin and West Germany made this less probable as it would trigger a Soviet–American conflict, it remained a possibility, especially as the East Germans already had a 60,000-strong paramilitary 'peoples police' organised into 'alert units'.

Stalin was testing President Truman's resolve to contain communism behind its 1945 frontiers and the strength of its commitment to allies. If the US had not taken the initiative for a United Nations resistance to North Korea and sent US forces, then it would have appeared weak and timid compared to the USSR and undermined NATO, only created the year before in 1949, as West Europeans would feel they too would be abandoned in a crisis. American intelligence sources had warned Washington of an impending invasion yet it became the 'Pearl Harbour' of the Cold War because the intelligence was discounted (as in December 1941) for not fitting the Pentagon's preconceived notion that Stalin would only launch an invasion when he wanted to start World War III. Accordingly the Pentagon had no plans for sending troops to South Korea, no plans for a 'flexible response' in a 'limited war', only plans for dropping atom bombs. American soldiers were rushed to South Korea from bases in the US and Japan.

Stalin meant Korea to undermine NATO and the US position in Europe by diverting US attention and troops away from Europe to Asia. In fact it had the opposite effect. The Korean War globalised Truman's containment policy and militarised containment in Europe. In June 1950 the Americans wanted a stronger local defence of Western Europe to deter the USSR, including a West German contribution organised in a NATO integrated force under centralised command with a supreme commander. Seventy-five per cent of US military aid went to Europe even after the Korean War started. In 1950 there were only 14 runways from which jets could operate in Western Europe and only 800 jets to put on them: by 1954 there were 120 runways and 4,000 jets. American military aid helped re-equip the French air force and the RAF via 'off shore sales' (as opposed to 'legitimate off shore sales'). Some of the jet aircraft built in British and French factories were bought with US military aid and given to the air forces. These planes, paid for with dollars, were exports of a sort. Clement Attlee had announced a £3.6bn rearmament programme for 1951–54. By 1952 UK arms production exceeded all her European NATO partners combined – a fact that predisposed the US to give UK additional financial aid in 1952.

At the September 1950 NATO Council meeting in New York, Ernest Bevin had agreed both to Britain's contribution under revised NATO force goals rising to four divisions, and also with the American demand for the immediate creation of German formations under NATO command (Dockrill, 1989, p. 151). For the Americans, after June 1950, a German military contribution was indispensable to fill the big manpower gap at the centre of Western Europe's defence line. The Soviet threat made some restoration of West Germany's capacity for self-defence an urgent matter. Adenauer was keen to co-operate but at this time stopped short of a national German army and general staff. Adenauer in fact wanted a militarised police force of 150,000 men. Moreover, he wanted to anchor the FRG firmly in the Western camp, end occupation controls and regain full sovereignty. The US plan, backed by Britain, for German rearmament in NATO opened an intriguing possibility of an alternative and perhaps preferable route to these goals than via France's Schuman Plan. The German Social Democrats (SPD) were against any West German rearmament, wanting to see Germany reunified.

Robert Schuman when confronted at the New York NATO Summit in September 1950 with the prospect of a rapid reappearance of an independent German army flew into a rage full of anti-German invective. He argued in what was described as a lively and traumatic meeting that the whole issue of German rearmament should be postponed until the ECSC was in place. For Truman, the issue of adding West German manpower to Western Europe's defence was non-negotiable; it was clear according to Truman that

> without Germany the defence of Europe was a rearguard action on the shore of the Atlantic Ocean, with Germany there could be a defence in

depth, powerful enough to offer effective resistance to aggression from the East . . .

Moreover, this was essential and realistic given the heavy US military involvement in Korea, Britain's global military responsibilities and France fighting a colonial war in Indo-China.

The French government instructed Schuman not to yield. They resented the Americans trying to impose their own swift solution to the German problem through rearmament. Yet France was in too weak a position to prevent any determined American rearmament of Germany; they could only hope to complicate and delay the process.

Monnet, like Schuman, was also alarmed that this US scheme for German rearmament on a national basis in NATO would wreck the ECSC plan. Monnet wrote to Schuman in New York saying the only alternative was 'to integrate Germany into Europe by means of a broader Schuman Plan, taking the necessary decisions within a European framework' (Fursdon, 1980, pp. 84–5). German rearmament, only five years after the war, was a distasteful and alarming prospect for most Europeans, Russians and many Germans. For France it also jeopardised the Schuman Plan. If West Germany regained full sovereignty through a defence contribution to NATO they would be under American control and also be less motivated to proceed with the Schuman Plan on the agreed French terms.

Only a month before, on 11 August, Winston Churchill in the Council of Europe at Strasbourg had called for 'the immediate creation of a unified European army subject to proper democratic control and acting in full co-operation with the US and Canada'. Although Churchill envisaged a European army with a European Minister of Defence of 36 divisions (15 French, 6 British, 6 American, 5 West German, 3 Benelux), 17 per cent of the force would have been American (Dockrill, 1991, p. 24). The European Assembly enthusiastically endorsed Churchill's proposal, voting 85 to 5 in favour.

Churchill's idea inspired and the vote encouraged Monnet's Plan as did Adenauer's refusal to accept a German national army whilst welcoming the idea of an integrated force. The threat from a recon- structed German army, in any form, guaranteed French opposition to American plans. Monnet, chairman of the Schuman Plan team, after consulting Schuman and Pleven (the French Prime Minister), used the same team that was working on the Schuman Plan's continuing coal and steel conference, to devise a scheme for a European army. He deliberately excluded any military expertise, as the priority was to devise a political solution acceptable to France. By 14 October the essential elements of the 'Pleven Plan' were in place and following redrafting both the French Cabinet and the National Assembly had accepted the Pleven Plan by 24 October 1950 (Fursdon, 1980, pp. 86–8).

What did the original Pleven Plan propose? It aimed to create a European army with a European Defence Community, copying the institutional form of the ECSC. It was to be created once the ECSC Treaty had been signed. The EDC was to be linked to a European Political Community (EPC) that would exercise democratic control over the EDC. The EDC would have common forces, a common uniform and a single Ministry of Defence. However, Monnet and Pleven envisaged an EDC that was only ostensibly supranational as the 100,000 strong European army, including West Germans, was to contain a 50,000 strong French contingent. So the EDC was intended to be half French with the West German contingent controlled by French cadres. All participating states, except for West Germany, would retain national control over their forces not placed in the EDC. As Dockrill shows, French counter-proposals to American demands to rearm Germany in October 1950 were designed to deny them the opportunity for independent action and so from becoming a military threat again. Under the guise of supranationality, a *fusion complète* of military forces, France aimed to attain military superiority over West German forces organized into battalions of 1,000 men in the European army under French generals as the best insurance against any resurgence of German militarism and excessive American interference in European affairs. The Pleven Plan intended the European army to be dominated by France – under French command with a French Minister of Defence (Fursdon, 1980, pp. 89–90; Dockrill, 1989, pp. 153–4; 1991, p. 42).

The EDC appeared to the Dutch and British Foreign Ministers as a means of French national aggrandisement and a platform for French political hegemony. Four days after the French National Assembly had approved it, the French counter-proposal for solving the vexed question of German rearmament was presented at the Defence Committee meeting of western powers to consider how to incorporate German forces in European defence. The French initiative was generally welcomed as a positive alternative strategy based on Churchill's Strasbourg proposal in August. France was thus able to avoid complete isolation with her NATO partners on the issue, and also retain essential US support for France in its Schuman Plan negotiations with Germany. Dr Adenauer did not like the inherent discrimination against German forces in the French proposals nor the fact that achieving progress with the Pleven Plan was linked up and conditional upon the success of the Schuman Plan negotiations (the Treaty of Paris was signed in April 1951).

These two distinct solutions to German rearmament were debated inside NATO from the start of 1951. The Petersburg Conference in Bonn considered the 'Spofford Proposals' for German forces to be wholly integrated under the NATO command. This was the quick American military solution preferred by everyone except France. The Paris Conference considered the Pleven Plan that offered the possibility of a long-term political solution to the German problem through 'political unity in a community'. The Dutch (like the US and UK) remained as observers not participants at the Paris Conference as Dirk Stikker, the Dutch Foreign Minister, simply did not believe that the French were serious about the EDC or really prepared to relinquish any sovereignty over the French Army (Fursdon, 1980, pp. 91, 99, 105–9).

Dr Adenauer pursued a successful trade-off policy at these conferences. He wanted equality of treatment for the West Germans, and the price of German military co-operation with the West was West Germany's political independence. Negotiations on a new contractual relationship between the three western occupying powers and West Germany started in Bonn in May 1951. The West Germans insisted on having a Ministry of Defence, divisional formations and in return it was prepared to provide a ground force of 100,000 men by the end of 1951 (Dockrill, 1991, pp. 59–62). Moreover, the two-track NATO debate meant that concessions won by the FRG at the Petersburg Conference from January 1951 became prerequisites at the informal exploratory talks of the European Army Conference in Paris, February–June 1951. Here the West Germans insisted on the 'Bonn requirements' of equality and political independence.

West Germany was in a strong negotiating position at the Paris Conference (through the Bonn talks on new contractual agreements) and France was forced to make some very big concessions to retain German involvement at the European Army Conference including acceptance of a *fusion complète* (all forces being in EDC from the start) meaning the French army would cease to exist. If the West Germans had left these talks they were doomed and the NATO solution, a new West German army and a politically independent West Germany could follow.

The US had originally agreed to a Pleven Plan conference in Paris in late 1950 in return for the immediate remilitarisation of Germany on an interim basis. However, German demands for equality, talks on a new contractual agreement with Germany and the ongoing Paris Conference meant no swift rearmament on an interim basis. The Americans then began to look more favourably at the French scheme as a long-term solution to German rearmament.

Monnet lobbied hard with US officials visiting or based in Europe. He was well connected with the US political establishment, particularly the State Department in Washington, and Europe. John McCloy, the US High Commissioner in West Germany and David Bruce, US Ambassador in Paris, were both good friends of Monnet and also convinced Euro-federalists. Over lunch in the Waldorf-Astoria in Paris, Monnet converted Eisenhower to the French Plan. Monnet told Eisenhower, NATO's commander, that

> to rush into raising a few German divisions on a national basis, at the cost of reviving enmity between our peoples would be catastrophic for the very security of Europe it was intended to ensure,

whereas the French approach was a community approach encouraging a common European interest in defence and a will to resist. Eisenhower's views, as NATO's Supreme Commander, were transformed, 'what Monnet's proposing is to organize relations between people and I'm all for it'. Eisenhower threw his weight behind the Paris Conference and defended the European army idea (that he once considered 'crazy and impractical') staunchly before the Senate Sub-Committee on Foreign Relations in July 1951. Konrad Adenauer seeing the way US policy was moving also put his support behind the Paris Conference. Dean Acheson, US Secretary of State, was eventually persuaded by these developments and by David Bruce to switch American policy from the Petersburg NATO solution to going 'all out for' the EDC alternative at the Paris Conference. President Truman formally agreed to this on 30 July 1951. After protracted negotiations the vast Treaty of Paris of 27 May 1952 establishing the EDC was signed, having 132 articles and 12 protocols. A protocol to the NATO Treaty on reciprocal guarantees with EDC was signed. The Allied–German Contractual Agreement was signed in Bonn the previous day, 26 May 1952, to grant the Federal Republic 'full power over its domestic and foreign affairs' once the EDC came into effect. However, the real problem of getting parliamentary ratification in the six states, especially France, was only now beginning (Fursdon, 1980, pp. 117–21, 151; Dockrill, 1991, pp. 68–72).

What was Britain's attitude towards a European army? Britain always preferred a NATO solution to German rearmament. Anthony Eden, the Conservative Foreign Secretary from October 1951 to 1955, continued with the policy established by Ernest Bevin. Bevin indicated at the Labour Party Conference in September 1950 that he had no time for a European army. His response to the Pleven Plan on 29 November 1950 made clear that it was not the 'policy of His Majesty's Government to contribute United Kingdom forces to a European Army. . . Europe is not enough, it is not big enough' (House of Commons *Debates*, 29 Nov. 1950, vol. 481, col. 1175). Bevin for a time advocated an 'Atlantic Confederate Force' under the NATO Supreme Commander to counter the Pleven Plan for a European army. The Cabinet, suspecting that the US Congress would never agree to this, preferred the American idea of a NATO integrated force. At a NATO meeting in Washington in September 1951, Herbert Morrison, who took over when Bevin fell ill, announced that although the UK could not merge its forces in a European army, Britain fully supported the idea and wished to be closely associated with it (Dockrill, 1991, p. 49; Dedman and Fleay, 1992, p. 12).

Hopes were raised in Europe, only to be swiftly dashed, of a change in British government policy from October 1951. Winston Churchill became Conservative Prime Minister and Anthony Eden the Foreign Secretary. The Conservative Party included a group of 'Tory Strasbourgers' and the Cabinet contained several European-minded Ministers such as Duncan Sandys, David Patrick Maxwell-Fyfe and Harold Macmillan, who, partly inspired by Churchill's Zurich and Strasbourg speeches in 1946 and 1950, wanted to see a more decisive British lead in Europe. In November 1951, in what has been described as the 'betrayal of Strasbourg' or 'the Rome coup', Maxwell-Fyfe, the Home Secretary hand-picked by Eden, went to read a Cabinet-approved statement at the Council of Europe Assembly. This was a cautious though not discouraging statement concerning the UK and a European army and denied that there was any 'closing of the door' by Britain. That same evening, 28 November 1951, Eden, at a NATO meeting in Rome, slammed the door shut. He stated bluntly and categorically that the UK would not join a European army. When news of this reached Strasbourg, Paul-Henri Spaak, President of the European Assembly, resigned immediately. Maxwell-Fyfe was on the brink of resigning and was subsequently castigated and vilified in the British press for exceeding his brief. Although the statements arguably differed more in tone than substance, in reality Maxwell-Fyfe was not to blame. Eden had spoken the day before to General Eisenhower, who instead of urging the UK to join the EDC told him it would be a mistake. Eden explained to Churchill that Britain should support the EDC but offering to enter it at this stage of the negotiations 'would further complicate the budgetary and other technical arrangements and would delay rather than hasten a final solution'. Churchill replied on 29 November that Eden's position 'combined the

disadvantages of two courses: neither keeping out of it nor having a say'
(Young, 1985, pp. 928–9; Dockrill, 1991, pp. 85–8; Dedman and Fleay,
1992, p. 13).

This public divergence of view within the government did not help
Britain's standing on the Continent. Churchill had an emotional attach-
ment to both the US (he was half American) and to Europe. He was an
enthusiastic exponent of European schemes and although consistently
careful to say that Britain was 'with Europe not of it', he was prone to
spirited visionary prose on the matter. Eden, as Churchill's named
successor, shared none of these characteristics. To the chagrin of Tory-
Strasbourgers with their vague ideas of Britain playing its part in Europe,
Eden (who was described as 'in every sense a NATO man' by Anthony
Nutting of the Foreign Office) was having none of it.

On 6 December in the House of Commons, Churchill confirmed
Bevin's rejection of the EDC and Eden's line in saying that once formed 'a
European Army containing a German contribution . . . will stand
alongside the British and US armies in a common defensive front' (House
of Commons *Debates*, 6 Dec. 1951, vol. 494, col. 2591). Following a
meeting with Pleven, Schuman and Eisenhower in Paris on 18 December,
the Bevin–Morrison–Eden policy was reaffirmed in the announcement
that Britain 'would associate (herself) as closely as possible with the EDC
in all stages of its political and military developments'.

Why did British policy adhere so consistently to a NATO solution, with
German rearmament in an Atlantic and not a European context between
1950–55? Britain was afraid that once the EDC was established the US,
satisfied that Europe was capable of self-defence, would be able to
withdraw its forces from Western Europe and Germany. Britain's policy,
even before the 1949 NATO Agreement came into effect, was based on
getting and keeping a permanent US military presence in Europe. The
UK would not consequently support or encourage anything that might
weaken this essential US commitment. The American policy was the
converse of Britain's in Western Europe. They wanted to deter the USSR
and contain any resurgence of German militarism without the need for
permanently stationing US forces there. The EDC seemed their best
solution. Once support for the EDC became US policy from July 1951 the
UK could not reject it outright and had to support it from outside (closest
possible association) and avoid any accusation of sabotage or responsibility if or when the EDC scheme failed (Dockrill, 1989, pp. 158, 161–4;
Mager, 1992, p. 127). Britain's refusal to join made the EDC's failure more
likely, as France felt uncomfortable in a *fusion complète* of its armed forces
with those of West Germany without the reassuring counterpoise of

British membership to any resurgence of German strength. The need to avoid responsibility for any EDC collapse prompted Britain to breathe some life into its policy of 'closest possible association' through a Declaration maintaining British troops in Europe; signing a Treaty with the EDC promising UK support if attacked; and close collaboration in training and joint exercises (Dockrill, 1989, p. 153; Young, 1988, ch. 3, p. 90; Mager, 1992, p. 127).

Avoiding blame for any EDC failure was important to Britain given the particularly close special relationship that existed in the Truman–Acheson era (and the risk that alienating the US Congress might prejudice votes on US military aid to Britain); it was ironic that the UK and US's aspirations for the EDC were diametrically opposed.

Britain was determined to avoid being in any pact which included Italy and West Germany but not the US – as it would be far harder to deal with any resurgent militarism with only rather weak European partners (Dockrill, 1989, p. 161; 1991, p. 2).

Britain's consistent policy towards the EDC had been to wait for the Pleven Plan originally and then the EDC Treaty to die (meanwhile keeping quiet about its NATO alternative) and then after its collapse to push for the UK's preferred NATO solution. The UK's response to the whole Pleven Plan/EDC scheme episode between 1951–55 was a cautious, patient waiting game (Young, 1988, ch. 3, p. 102; Dockrill, 1989, p. 167). The Foreign Office was determined to avoid the complex unwanted commitment that membership of a supranational EDC would bring. It would have constrained Britain's political and military independence while encouraging the development of a European federation. British Foreign Office observers at the EDC talks were mainly concerned to see if the EDC countries negotiated a better deal for military aid with the US than Britain already had – it soon became clear that they did not. Once the EDC was operable, rather like Marshall Aid and the OEEC, US military aid was to be 'pooled' and apportioned by the supranational EDC, a prospect that worried the Dutch a good deal. There was concern too by the British Foreign Office that when the FRG joined the EDC the £80m p. a. that Germany paid the UK to keep troops in Germany might cease. The immediate prospect for the Foreign Office, anxious about the balance of payments, was that the EDC could cost Britain £80m p. a. even though she was not a member.

For the French it was much more than a matter of money. France was opposed in principle to rearming Germany. The Pleven Plan and EDC were not attractive prospects, simply a lesser evil than a new Wehrmacht in NATO. France was torn between its need to integrate any German military forces into an EDC and its reluctance to integrate its own army. To most Frenchmen it seemed absurd to give arms to Germans when they did not appear to want them. (The West German Social Democrat Party resisted the issue of rearmament all the way to the FRG's Supreme Court.) It also appeared to represent the abandonment of a traditional ally, Britain, for too close an association with the ex-enemy. Hence the opposition slogans of 'No Europe without Britain', and 'The European Army destroys the French Army and rebuilds the German Army'.

Political opposition to the EDC in France was wide-ranging. The left wing of the Socialist Party was hostile to the rearmament of Germany. Nationalists were opposed to the dissolution of the French army and communists were opposed to the whole Atlantic policy. This opposition was a formidable alliance of left and right, including the communists and Gaullists. General de Gaulle, out of office, said at an RPF conference:

> The European Army plan would be either the end of the French Army or just a smoke screen which would permit the resurrection of the German Army without the least guarantee of its use. It would be a fatal blow to the French Army. We alone would be surrendering our army. To whom? To Europe? But it does not exist. We would be giving it to General Eisenhower. For centuries our value and prestige have been merged with those of the French Army. We therefore must not and cannot give up an army of our own.

These were views that were widely shared in France. The US hoped for speedy ratification of the EDC Treaty after May 1952 but Schuman felt that there was no majority in the National Assembly to vote it into law. Over the next two years three more French governments claimed to support the EDC but failed to ratify it. Other states postponed doing so too because of French delays.

Why was the Pleven Plan acceptable to the French National Assembly but the EDC Treaty, 18 months later, thought not to be? The Pleven Plan was widely recognised in October 1950 as a device to stop, not create, something. It was intended to prevent instant German rearmament and to protect the basic bargain that lay behind the Schuman Plan. The Milan journal, *Relazioni Internazionali* (December 1950) recognised this, questioning whether the Pleven Plan represented 'truly supranational motives or the mere tactical desire to control German rearmament'. (The EDC Treaty, unlike the Pleven Plan, was not a sketchy scheme hastily devised in less than a month.) If the EDC was ratified a European army, including German soldiers, would come into existence and members' national armies would cease to exist. Moreover, German forces could then be stationed throughout the community, for example in France or Holland.

The EDC Treaty differed substantially from what was originally envisaged in the Pleven Plan. The Pleven Plan intended the European Army to be half French, the US Spofford Plan envisaged the German contribution to NATO forces to be one fifth, and under the EDC Treaty 1952 the European army was to be one-third German (Dockrill, 1991, p. 55). The West Germans insisted on the principle of absolute equality in the European army and so, unlike the Pleven Plan, France came to agree to a *fusion complète* with all members' forces integrated into the EDC from the start. Moreover, the Pleven Plan was from the outset inherently flawed in a crucial respect, in envisaging German *groupements* being no bigger than a brigade or regimental combat teams. The French objected to there being German divisions, and even to the use of the word. This, however, was eventually acknowledged to be impractical militarily and logistically (*groupements* were ultimately intended to be small divisions of 13,000 men). It meant there would have to be a German War Office to organise these German divisions, which also meant it would be possible to re-form a German General Staff. The whole point and purpose of the Pleven Plan was to avoid this (Dockrill, 1991, pp. 71, 89, 48–9).

The Pleven Plan envisaged a French General being in overall command of a European army but instead, under the EDC, a Board of Commissioners, including German members, was to run it. Article 15 set the quorum at five of the nine commissioners, voting on a majority basis (Fursdon, 1980, p. 155; Dockrill, 1991, p. 42).

Articles 9–16 of the EDC Treaty which dealt with the withdrawal of troops from the EDC for use elsewhere, placed unwelcome constraints on French colonial rule and national sovereignty. However, it was Article 43 that worried the French the most. This stated that member states' votes in the EDC Council were weighted by the size of their national contribution to the EDC. More soldiers meant more votes. Whilst unanimity applied to key matters, on a day-to-day basis Article 43 applied. Assuming the Treaty was ratified by January 1952, France was to have 14 *groupements*, Italy and Germany 12 each, and Benelux six in place by July 1954 (Fursdon, 1980, pp. 158, 199; Dockrill, 1991, p. 89).

The problem was that the demand on French military manpower, due to its colonial war in Indo-China, meant that in February 1952 France decided to reduce her number of *groupements* in the EDC from 14 to ten. It chose to do this rather than to send conscripts to fight in Indo-China or to extend conscription to two years (as in the UK) and as promised to NATO in 1950 (Dockrill, 1991, p. 107).

This meant France, with ten *groupements*, would have fewer votes under Article 43 compared with Rome and Bonn who had 12 each. Given Germany's undoubted military expertise (1939–45) and the restoration of their economic strength from 1950, this meant that West Germany would dominate the EDC. Moreover a Board of Commissioners, not a French General, would run it and, unlike France, West Germany was not distracted or weakened by problems of decolonisation.

This was entirely the wrong result, the very reverse of the Pleven Plan and almost wholly unacceptable and unsellable politically in France. The Dutch too, who had been reluctant participants at the start, were concerned originally that the ECSC plus the EDC would be a platform for French hegemony in Western Europe. By 1952 both France and all three Benelux States were worried that a supranational EDC would not stop the resumption of German dominance.

Such misgivings resulted in delays to parliamentary ratification of the EDC Treaty and to increased pressure on the UK to participate or to provide binding guarantees to the EDC. In an effort to reassure EDC signatories the ECSC Assembly agreed on 10 September 1952 to devise plans for the EPC to cover the ECSC and EDC, as allowed for under Article 38 of the EDC Treaty. Alcide de Gasperi, Italy's Prime Minister, had inserted this clause because of his federalist beliefs and to allay the fears of the small states of domination by the big ones. By March 1953 the draft plan allowed for a bicameral parliament – a senate representing the six states and a popularly elected assembly – to provide for political control over both the EDC and ECSC. Eden's alternative idea, which would not have had to wait for EDC ratification, was to adapt the existing machinery of the Council of Europe for the ECSC and eventually the EDC too. This would permit close UK political 'association' with both bodies and allow the six members to vote on defence, coal, and steel issues with non-members as participant observers. Eden's initiative of a fast track to a political authority was rejected by 'Little Europe' in favour of the Article 38 route. Monnet, too, saw this Eden Plan as a threat to the ECSC's independence (Fursden, 1980, pp. 213–14).

In January 1953 the US government changed: Eisenhower became the first Republican President for 20 years, with John Foster Dulles as his Secretary of State. They were determined to speed up progress with EDC ratification. The French were blamed for delays and prevarication, and the UK for lack of vigour and a lukewarm diplomacy in pushing for the EDC. In January 1953 Dulles threatened 'a little rethinking on Europe' to hasten developments. Between March and June 1953 this became the threat of the US reverting to a 'peripheral strategy' (a US withdrawal from Western Europe except for bases in Spain, UK and Iceland). These threats were directed at France particularly because of mounting US impatience with delays in ratification.

However, the actual prospects for EDC ratification deteriorated when Stalin died on 5 March 1953, and the USSR seemed less menacing as Malenkov, his successor, appeared more moderate. The Korean War, which started the saga of West German rearmament, ended in an armistice signed on 27 July 1953. In May 1953 Churchill called for a summit conference with Malenkov to end the Cold War. This strength-ened opponents of German rearmament providing an excellent excuse for delaying ratification. Malenkov's 'peace offensive' aimed to under-mine the process of West European military integration and German rearmament by Soviet proposals for a 'neutralised' united Germany (Young, 1986, pp. 889–95; Fish, 1986, pp. 333–4).

By December 1953 American exasperation with French delays to ratification and annoyance with Churchill's proposal for four-power talks with the Russians before the EDC was in place meant renewed pressure from the Americans. Eden was warned by Dulles in December 1953 of an 'agonising reappraisal' of US defence commitments if the EDC failed. Dulles threatened to swing over to 'hemispheric defence', abandoning Europe and putting Asia first. Eden told Dulles that the French were 'impervious to cajolery or the prospect of dire alternatives', and urged the NATO solution for German rearmament should the EDC fail.

Eden, unlike the French, did not dismiss this threat as a complete bluff. On 12 December 1953 he wrote to the Minister of Defence urging him to consider the possibility of putting a UK unit into the EDC as he was 'convinced we were at a turning point in the whole relationship of the US to Europe and we must have recourse to all our imagination and ingenuity to help the EDC through'. Eden faced a dilemma. If the EDC passed it might facilitate US withdrawal from Europe (once West German troops were in place). Dulles now threatened withdrawal if the EDC failed.

Why were the French impervious to such US threats? France was much more concerned with the German question than the Russian threat and could only gain by delay. If France had attempted to ratify the Treaty in the National Assembly, and by some miracle it passed, a European army would have been created, with West Germany rearmed and the French army disbanded. If the EDC failed in the Chamber the Anglo-Americans could then have rearmed Germany via the NATO solution. Only through delaying ratification did France gain by effectively freezing the whole issue of German rearmament and the restoration of full sovereignty to West Germany.

The French were immune to Dulles' bullying for three other reasons. France was logistically crucial to the US and NATO defence strategy for Western Europe. US bases in France and French troops in NATO made France a vital ally for America. Second, the vagaries of the French party political and parliamentary systems, under the constitution of the Fourth Republic 1946–58, meant that foreign governments had to deal with eight French coalition governments during the lifetime of the European army scheme 1950–54, and seven different Prime Ministers, although only three different Foreign Ministers (Williams, 1954, p. 440, Appendix 3).

Finally, France was engaged in a colonial war in Indo-China against the Vietminh, struggling for national liberation with Chinese communist support. For Eisenhower and Dulles France was at the frontline containing the spread of communism in Indo-China. By 1954 the US was funding 80 per cent of the cost of France's colonial war: some $800m on supporting France in Indo-China, amounting to a third of the total US military aid budget. France was desperate to extricate itself from Indo-China and the US was very concerned that France might simply throw in the towel and abandon the struggle. This would have been a major setback for US foreign policy and influence in Asia. Eisenhower in his memoirs complained that the French were always 'tying the fate of the EDC to our willingness to do things in Indo-China as the French government desired'. The military situation in Indo-China was deteriorating rapidly from February 1954, and the US sent 400 US Air Force mechanics and light bombers to support French forces there. Dulles at the Berlin Conference (of the UK, US, USSR and French Foreign Ministers) in January–February 1954, had very reluctantly agreed to support Laniel's (the French Prime Minister) and Bidault's urgent request for a conference on Indo-China to end the war. This was agreed with Molotov, the Soviet Foreign Minister, at Berlin and scheduled for Geneva in April. Dulles gave way on this because he believed Laniel would swiftly ratify the EDC Treaty, and felt betrayed when this did not happen.

Between January and April 1954 four states ratified the EDC Treaty; only France and Italy had not done so (Dockrill, 1991, p. 139). For Dulles, Soviet intransigence at the Berlin Conference made the EDC indispensable but events there, in Indo-China and in France, reduced the prospects of attainment.

Molotov, at the Berlin Conference, had contrived to publicise a clause in the Bonn Contractual Agreements, stating that any future unified Germany would be free to withdraw from the EDC as it was not bound by the obligations of the FRG. French opponents of the EDC fastened on this fact, further reducing chances of ratification.

For France, pre-occupied both with ending its Indo-China crisis and the fate of besieged French defenders at Dien Bien Phu, it meant there was little prospect of ratification until the outcome of both the conference and the battle were known. Paradoxically, the European army plan that was born in Korea was to die in Indo-China. Anthony Eden said 'the fate of the EDC was in part dependent on a solution in Indo-China' (Eden, 1960, p. 84).

Ratification in France was delayed further by the Foreign Affairs Committee of the National Assembly examining the Treaty until April, and by Laniel when Gaullists insisted on various preconditions being met including UK and US guarantees to the EDC and even the settlement of the future of the Saar-land (Laniel's government included two Gaullist ministers and was dependent in part on Gaullist support). Opponents of the EDC were encouraged by the Juin Affair on 28 March 1954. Marshall Juin, Permanent Military Adviser to the French Government and Vice-President of the Supreme Council of the Armed Forces, was sacked for gross insubordination for saying in a speech to Reserve Officers that an alternative solution to the European army 'could and should be found'.

In the context of a worsening Indo-China crisis and mounting opposition to the EDC in France, Eden announced to the House of Commons on 14 April the Agreement on British co-operation with the EDC (signed in Paris the previous day). Eden said Britain was ready to place a British armoured division, stationed in Germany, within an EDC Corps and under EDC command when the Treaty came into effect (House of Commons *Debates*, 1953–54, vol. 526, cols. 1142–5). This offer came too late to sway French opinion in favour of the EDC. Eden had warned Sir Christopher Steel, UK delegate at the Paris EDC talks, of this a month before but had told him not to reveal it to the French 'as it might only induce them to ask for more or for a written guarantee'. Eden's announcement was well received in the US and by it he hoped to avoid any blame for the probable demise of the scheme. Under Dulles' threat of 'agonising reappraisal' and the need to prevent the UK being the scapegoat for the EDC's failure, Eden offered a division of tanks for the European army. The timing was well judged – it came too late to improve the chance of ratification in France.

The Geneva Conference on Indo-China started on 26 April 1954 (where Eden and Molotov were co-chairmen). The long expected fall of

Dien Bien Phu occurred on 7 May 1954 when the last French Legionnaire defenders surrendered, finally overrun by the Vietminh's human wave assaults. Laniel survived an immediate vote of confidence but his government fell on 12 June during the Indo-China Debate. On 16 June the forthcoming Washington Talks (scheduled for 25–26 June 1954) between the UK and US were announced. These informal talks were intended to repair Anglo-American relations which had been turbulent and badly damaged by the Geneva Conference. Eden and Dulles had had at least two rows in recent weeks. Dulles was furious that Britain refused to back American plans for 'united action' in support of the French in Indo-China and had to abandon the idea of military intervention there (bombing the hills around Dien Bien Phu and sending in Divisions of US marines). Eden was subsequently accused of appeasement of communist China and his efforts at diplomatic brokerage between parties at Geneva were, he felt, misrepresented by US State Department officials and the American press as creating a 'Far Eastern Munich'. Dulles in a speech at Los Angeles on 11 June 1954 made pointed references to Britain's faint-heartedness.

Commenting on the forthcoming Washington Talks the French newspaper *Le Monde*, on 17 June 1954, in the absence of a French government, referred to the humiliation of France:

> because the two main questions for discussion at Washington will be Indo-China and German rearmament in which French interest is second to none . . . and that the Prime Minister (Churchill) will have a new opportunity to plead for an autonomous wehrmacht and may meet less American opposition than he did at Bermuda.

(The Bermuda Conference was in early December 1953 between France, UK and US.)

The weekend talks in Washington marked a rapprochement in Anglo-American relations. Agreement was reached on Eden's solution for Indo-China of partition along the 17th Parallel, establishing a joint 'study group' to consider alternatives to the EDC should it fail as well as a timetable for getting the EDC or alternative solutions through before November's mid-term elections in the United States. The US and UK seized the initiative over the EDC away from France as the Geneva Conference was moving towards an agreement. French diplomats two weeks later, in July, complained of an 'organised campaign of pressure against France', and of leaked 'hypothetical alternative policies' to the EDC (such as a return to Bizonia without France!) (Public Record Office (PRO), FO 371/112781, 7 July 1954).

It was recognised in the capitals of 'Little Europe', London and Washington, that once Laniel's government had gone there was no chance of a self-declared pro-EDC candidate winning an absolute majority of the National Assembly's votes (314) needed for investiture as Prime Minister. On 19 June 1954 Mendès-France (with 419 votes) became the first French Premier since 1952 not to commit himself to ratification but to promise a vote by a certain date. His government composed of Radicals and Gaullist ministers, was split on the EDC issue. The Socialist Party who voted him into office and called for ratification of the Treaty also refused to participate in his government! He was the first Prime Minister since 1947 that the Communist Party (99 votes) voted into office – sensing the end of the EDC.

On 23 July Mendès-France's Indo-China settlement was approved by the National Assembly but on the issue of the EDC Mendès-France announced that his government was 'united only on one point namely that they disagreed completely with everyone else' (PRO FO 800/790, FR/54/5, 6 August 1954). Mendès-France pressed his allies for a two-month delay before putting the EDC to the vote as it was likely to fail so soon after the Indo-China settlement. Churchill, in a note to Eden, opposed any further postponements as they would 'alter the whole timetable for fulfilling the Bonn Convention as agreed by us with Ike in Washington' (PRO FO 800/779, EN/54/15).

On 6 August Mendès-France wanted to renegotiate the whole EDC Treaty, with complete disregard for the position of the Benelux and German governments, who had already ratified the treaty. Mendès-France wanted to remove the supranational components and equality of rights for Germany in the Treaty and in effect create 'a European Army for the Germans and a French Army for France'. Italy, poised to ratify the Treaty, backed off from doing so in the face of these French proposals. The disappointment and shock apparently killed Alcide de Gasperi, the Italian ex-Prime Minister (Fursdon, 1980, pp. 269, 280, 284–5). At the Brussels Conference on 19 August 1954, Mendès-France met to argue his case with the other EDC states. It was rejected as wholly unacceptable. Following this conference Mendès-France visited Churchill at Chartwell, who told him the Western Bloc 'could not agree to be governed by the impotence of the French Chamber in which we have no vote' (Kirkpatrick, 1959, p. 261). Yet Churchill also hinted to Mendès-France that Britain would pursue an alternative solution should the EDC fail, which was of some encouragement. Churchill also telegrammed Dulles after this meeting to report that Mendès-France was

much keener about NATO. . . as France would not be boxed up in civil
and military affairs with a more active and powerful West Germany,
whereas in the NATO system, the UK and US counter-balance
Germany to proper proportions.
(Fursdon 1980, p. 292; PRO FO 800/790 FR/54/28, 24 Aug. 1954)

Following the Brussels Conference few realistically expected the EDC
to survive a vote; it was generally discounted as a 'dead duck' by US State
Department officials briefing the American press. On 30 August 1954 the
long saga of the EDC ended; it died in the French National Assembly
without even being accorded the dignity of a debate; a technical motion
was passed to proceed to other business. Communists and Gaullist
deputies got to their feet and sang *La Marseillaise* amid general uproar.
Mendès-France abstained and his government remained neutral – it was
not made an issue of confidence and was therefore not a resigning matter
if it failed (Fursdon, 1980, pp. 296–7). Mendès-France stayed in office and
the EDC was buried. Laniel's government had paradoxically survived a
vote of confidence on the subject of a European army on 27 November
1953, which had encouraged Eisenhower and Dulles to believe in the
EDC's eventual ratification. However, the issue then was of confidence,
not the Treaty's ratification.

This French rejection of a French scheme was the cause of much
bitterness, resentment and disappointment in the capitals of 'Little
Europe' – and also in Washington. However, while generally regarded
as a diplomatic defeat for the US, it was not a domestic political issue.
Democrats and Republicans were similarly distressed. Dulles described it
as a 'serious set back' and a 'tragedy' and said:

US post war policies were framed on the assumption that Western
Europe would at long last develop a unity which would make it
immune from war between its members and defensible against
aggression from without.

(PRO FO 371/10901 28 Aug.–4 Sept. 1954)

In London, Washington and Bonn there had for some months been a
growing apprehension regarding Konrad Adenauer's political future.
French delays and prevarication had jeopardised his western-orientated
policy's survival and increased the danger of Germany drifting towards
'nationalism and neutrality' because of the political strain of enduring the
agony of the EDC's living death. After 30 August the German predicament became an urgent matter (borne out by the Schleswig-Holstein
September election results – seen as a rebuff to Adenauer's policy on the

EDC) as the Bonn Contractual Agreement had collapsed along with the EDC and its associated plans, under Article 38, for an EPC. It was widely anticipated in the press that Britain and America would now restore German sovereignty and obtain a German contribution to defence even against French opposition.

After what Eden referred to as 'the entangling impediment' of the EDC was dead, he took the initiative to pursue Britain's preferred NATO solution for German rearmament and restoration of German sovereignty. The Americans had no alternative to the EDC prepared. Eden's plan, which he claimed he thought of in the bath, was to use the Brussels Treaty of 1948. An enlarged Brussels Treaty Organization (BTO) – renamed Western European Union – would make West Germany's absorption into NATO more acceptable to France, providing a figleaf of political control as Britain and France were already members of the BTO. It was a non-supranational consultative body and Germany and Italy could be equal members. Dockrill has shown that, in fact, it was an old idea (Eden had mentioned it in Cabinet in December 1952). Eden's plan won UK Cabinet approval on 27 August 1954 (Fursdon, 1980, p. 313; Dockrill, 1991, p. 146).

Eden on 11 September embarked on his whirlwind diplomacy, making a flying circuit of Brussels, Bonn, Rome and Paris. His Brussels plan solution was received with some relief in the first three. Eden, in Paris, impressed on Mendès-France the dangers of driving Germany into the arms of Russia and the US into 'fortress America' (PRO FO 371/109101). Mendès-France subsequently announced the Brussels solution as his own idea.

On 28 September 1954 a nine-power conference started at Lancaster House, London, to resolve finally the vexed linked issues of German rearmament and restoration of German sovereignty based on Eden's plan. At the right psychological moment, Eden committed Britain's four divisions and the tactical air force stationed in West Germany to stay permanently in NATO for 50 years (and not to withdraw them without WEU approval). This was a commitment he had declined to give to the EDC, when requested by Schuman, in March 1954. Adenauer agreed to the 'ABC weapons policy' – of Germany not producing atomic, bacteriological and chemical weapons. France finally gave up her 'prolonged resistance against Germany's entry into NATO' (Fursdon, 1980, p. 325; Young, 1988, ch. 3, p. 99; Dockrill, 1991, pp. 146–50). Dulles pledged US support. Thirty-three days after the French rejection of the EDC, accords were signed in London and Paris resolving the joint issues of rearmament and restoration of sovereignty for Germany. Thanks to

Eden's statecraft Dulles could stage the first televised 'Cabinet meeting' at the White House to draw national attention to this foreign policy success (after setbacks with Indo-China and the EDC) as part of the mid-term Republican election campaign.

By 5 May 1955 the ratification process was completed (it still took two attempts in the French National Assembly in December 1954). West Germany attained full sovereignty, with the termination of the last vestiges of the allied occupation regime, and the new Bundeswehr entered NATO.

Once German rearmament in NATO was an accomplished fact it ceased to be a political issue in France. This also applied to the USSR. In 1955 West Germany and the USSR exchanged ambassadors.

A postscript to the 1950s European army scheme was the Franco-German plan for developing the WEU into a separate European defence pillar in autumn 1991, prior to the Maastricht European Council meeting. Britain's reaction was a faithful echo of her 1950s policy, insisting that any proposed WEU force should be autonomous, within NATO and outside EC control, 'linked to both and subordinated to neither'. Britain still did not want closer European co-operation to interfere with NATO nor encourage US withdrawal.

The eventual resolution of German rearmament confirms the substance of the old saw that 'NATO is all about keeping the Russians out, the Germans down, the Americans in and the French calm'.

The final irony for France was that it was not the Bundeswehr but the French army that proved the greater menace to the Fourth Republic in May 1958 (the threat of a military uprising code-named 'Resurrection' assisted General de Gaulle's return to power).

Why should so much attention be paid to an unsuccessful scheme? The EDC episode has a wider historical significance concerning the scope and motives for European integration. Nothing like it has been tried since. The hastily conceived European Union Treaty of 1992 did not attempt to recreate anything like the EPC or EDC. The only successful integration for 45 years has been economic. This suggests that the parameters for viable integration are fairly narrow – precluding, to date, non-economic supranational schemes.

The EDC is generally portrayed as an over-ambitious project in too sensitive an area that collapsed because it was such an idealistic and premature attempt at integration. However, was it a real attempt at integration or a French device for delay? The EDC may have collapsed but did it fail? From the standpoint of French national interests and security the outcome of the entire Pleven Plan–EDC episode, 1950–55, was not a failure at all. Fursdon, in conclusion, saw the EDC as 'the French device for keeping Germany out of NATO' (Fursdon, 1980, p. 337). It successfully delayed German rearmament and joining NATO for almost five years. Moreover, the European army scheme protected the Schuman Plan and embryonic ECSC as it prevented the restoration of German sovereignty by another means. The fact that the EDC and Bonn Agreements were inextricably linked meant that France managed to prevent the restoration of full German sovereignty between 1950–55. Why was this important to the ECSC's success? When it came into effect economic controls over German coal and steel were to end and France promised to press for the disbandment of the International Authority of the Ruhr. However, if Germany had regained its sovereignty by supplying troops to NATO, as the US proposed in September 1950, this might well have destroyed any German interest in the ECSC or at best weakened the French negotiating position. Would West Germany have made economic concessions to France in the ECSC if she had less to gain politically?

The ECSC Treaty did not complete ratification until August 1952 and its Common Market only started to operate fully in 1953. The ECSC's supranational High Authority and other components were untried experimental arrangements. So French control over the restoration of full sovereignty through the EDC Treaty provided some political insurance for the ECSC throughout the early 1950s. It would obviously be fallacious to impute French motives for creating the EDC between 1950–52 based only on evidence of its failure in 1954–55. Nevertheless it was the case that only by postponing ratification, by not putting the Treaty to the vote in the National Assembly, could France prevent German rearmament and the restoration of full sovereignty, as after a vote, and regardless of the result, German rearmament and full powers would certainly follow, either through the EDC or the NATO solution.

What are the implications of the EDC's collapse for Lipgens and Milward's explanations of European integration? Lipgens' view of the 1950s integration was that governments were putting European federalist ideas 'partly into effect', but there is no evidence for this at all (only the Americans and Italians were really interested in the prospects for political federation). The EDC episode revealed governments pursuing their own rather different national objectives and interests through diplomacy and bargaining, not co-operating together to construct an idealised conception of a federal Europe. Adenauer's overriding objective was the re-emergence of a fully independent West German state: this was achieved and permitted through the architectural framework of the ECSC and the NATO/WEU solution.

The parallel sagas of the ECSC and EDC 1950–54 tend to confirm

Milward's thesis that only economic integration is successful. Economic integration only occurs when nation states' economic plans and prospects depend on links with the West German economy. The Pleven Plan 1950, however, was conceived as a means to stop the American demand for swift West German rearmament and to protect the back of the Schuman Plan, which in turn was devised to safeguard the essential elements of the Monnet Plan. Military and civil integration as envisaged in the EDC Treaty was not an attractive political option in the early 1950s. Had the EDC come into force the supranational Board of Commissioners would decide where to deploy troops – German conscripts could have been stationed in France, Belgium and Holland.

Eden and the Foreign Office thought the end of the EDC and success of the 'Brussels Pact solution' for West German rearmament was a setback to 'federalists' and for supranational schemes in Western Europe. This was a major miscalculation. The demise of the EDC finally cleared the way for further negotiations on European economic integration. In fact, without the obstacle of the EDC they would probably have started much sooner.

In May 1955 West German sovereignty was restored and the WEU came into force, and in June the Messina Talks were held by the six 'Little Europe' states to consider establishing two new communities.

# Chapter 6

# From the Common Market to a Single Market
## The Treaties of Rome (1957) to the Treaty on European Union (1992)

British hopes of stopping 'federalist' moves in Europe with the European Defence Community's failure and the success of the Western European Union were immediately quashed. Even before the ink was dry on the agreements concerning German sovereignty, in Paris in October 1954, parallel Franco-German negotiations were underway on their further economic co-operation or association. These included the possibility of German investment in the French Union (the French equivalent of the Commonwealth). By November 1954 the Americans were pressing 'Little Europe' to turn the WEU into a single trading area, an economic 'United States of Europe'. They envisaged a two-tier economic and political structure to balance the military unification of the WEU. One tier would be a 'Little Europe' of the six states, the other would be the UK with eventually perhaps the Scandinavians and others joining. (The stock reaction of the US to the creation of a new European organisation – as seen previously with the OEEC and EPU – was to try and widen its scope.)

British Foreign Office officials feared these initiatives might lead to the UK's exclusion from Europe and to a trade war with a new superstate, created under American and German auspices, while British forces were committed to its defence under NATO and the WEU. Four years later, in January 1958, under the Treaty of Rome, the European Economic Community (EEC) started to operate. Although far from being a superstate, Britain had indeed chosen to stay out of the EEC while its army and tactical airforce in West Germany defended its frontiers (*European Review*, 49, November 1954; 50, December 1954).

What exactly did the Treaties of Rome entail and how did this situation arise? The Treaties were signed by the six 'Little Europe' states on 25 March 1957. These established the EEC, a common market in manufactured goods with a Common Agricultural Policy (CAP) and Euratom – a common market in nuclear materials providing equal access to stocks of uranium 233. The Treaty of Rome establishing the EEC with its 248 articles, protocols and appendices was, none the less, mainly a statement of intent, a programme of action, a timetable. It was not a detailed comprehensive blueprint of regulations, as there simply had not been enough time for the necessary detailed micro-planning and negotiations between June 1955 and March 1957. The EEC came into force on 1 January 1958 with a completion date set for full operation of 31 December 1969. The Treaty's actual provisions often consisted of general statements concerning objectives and intentions where the details would have to be worked on and agreed in the future. The original Treaty of 177 pages contained only five on agriculture and Article 43 concerning a common agricultural policy occupied less than one page – although the eventual CAP was to consume more than two-thirds of the EEC budget by the late 1970s. The Treaty of Rome actually left virtually everything to be done. It did not automatically deliver a common market but relied on governments to reach agreement later. The EEC spent the first year of its official existence setting up shop in Brussels and getting its administrative machinery working. By the end of 1958 it had designed an ambitious programme for economic and commercial expansion in Europe, and common welfare and social policy objectives. The removal of tariffs and quantity restrictions by the six to create a single common market was to take place in three stages of four years each, starting in 1958. In the first stage tariffs were to be reduced by 30 per cent, in the second four years by 60 per cent and abolished completely by the end of the third stage. All export subsidies, export taxes and revenue duties on imports had to go before the end of the first stage. Although there were difficult negotiations between 1958–60 regarding the internal trade of the Common Market, tariff cuts were made ahead of the Treaty's scheduled timetable. By the end of 1960 tariff cuts already amounted to 30 per cent, while at the end of 1963 a 60 per cent cut had been agreed. In 1961 the removal of all quotas on imports was speeded up so that all quantity restrictions on imports enforced by EEC members were abolished.

The administrative structure of the EEC was very similar to the ECSC. The three communities, the ECSC, EEC and Euratom, shared the same Assembly – now called the European Parliament – and Court of Justice. Since 1967 they have had a common Council of Ministers and Commission, so that the three communities were fused into one with a common set of institutions.

Although the preamble to the Treaty of Rome 1957 reaffirmed their determination 'to establish the foundations of an ever closer union among the European peoples', following the failure of the EDC the word 'federalism' was never mentioned. For the EEC emphasis was placed on short- and medium-term economic and commercial benefits rather than long-term political possibilities to avoid arousing the latent fears of nationalists. It was essentially a commercial treaty between six states embedded in another supranational community.

Two institutions were of crucial importance to this community. The Commission of the EEC was the central concept behind the integrated organisation of the EEC. The architect of this was Pierre Uri, a French economist and colleague of Jean Monnet. The Commission had a multifunctional purpose and role, it acted as the EEC's executive civil service and it espoused the communities' interest (commissioners took an oath to pursue community and not national interests). The commissioners' main role was to initiate policy ('the Commission proposes but the Council disposes'). It was also the guardian of the Treaties – an important policing role to avoid systemic collapse through non-compliance, ensuring that members kept their obligations by mediating between members' interests and the Treaties' rules. The EEC's Commission had no national equivalent, being much more than a neutral bureaucratic executive. Indeed, it was initially regarded by many as the 'engine' of the EEC and 'an ever closer union'. The nine-man Commission to run the EEC with Professor Walter Hallstein as its first President, was different from the ECSC's High Authority in a number of respects.

The six states wanted to retain as much power as possible in their own hands and take all major decisions on proposals originating from the Commission through the EEC's Council of Ministers. Decision-making power lay collectively with 'the Six' – France, West Germany, Italy and Benelux. The Commission and the Council of Ministers together constituted the supranational integrated element in the Rome Treaties. The six member states transferred decisions concerning the Common Market and atomic energy to a supranational Council of Ministers drawn from the six states whose decisions were binding on all and had to be followed.

Unlike the ECSC's High Authority the six countries reserved the right to name their own commissioners, so in the EEC they were national nominees. The Commission also was wholly dependent on financial contributions from member states (until 1970) whereas the High Authority of the ECSC was financially autonomous through its own sales taxes. The EEC's Commission exercised less power than Monnet's High Authority of the ECSC (the original Schuman plan for an ECSC did not even include a Council of Ministers). By 1957 Monnet's High Authority was considered too powerful by France and Belgium.

The European Parliament was never a legislature: it has not passed a law since it started in 1952 as the assembly of the ECSC. Between 1958–75 it had to be consulted by the Council of Ministers which was then free to ignore it. The Parliament could also dismiss en masse the Commission voting with a two-thirds majority, a drastic but somewhat empty political check as national governments, not the Parliament, would have made the reappointments. Since 1970 the EP has won more budgetary control over EEC non-compulsory expenditure (the CAP, coming under the Treaty of Rome 1957 and representing 70 per cent of the budget in 1980, was 'compulsory' and so excluded). In 1975 an Amendment Treaty enabled the EP to reject the EEC budget as a whole which has occurred a number of times. A Court of Auditors was established in 1977 due to the EP's demand for a closer audit of EEC expenditure. In 1979 the first direct elections to the EP were held (previously representatives were sent by members' parliaments).

The Treaty of the European Union on 7 February 1992, in a gesture towards reducing the 'democratic deficit', gave the EP the power of 'co-decision' with the Council of Ministers over a limited number of issues (EU Treaty 1992, Article 189b) on internal market law, policies of research and development, training, education, health, consumer affairs. However, the key policies of agriculture (66 per cent of budget by 1986), fishing, foreign policies, competition and regional policies were all excluded. The EP since 1992 can 'request' the Commission to submit any proposal it wants where it considers new legislation is needed (EU Treaty 1992, Article 138b); whether the Commission is obliged to accede to such requests is another matter. While the EU Treaty also established an ombudsman, gave the EP more investigative powers and made the appointment of Commissioners and President subject to EP approval, these gains were mainly at the Commission's expense. Power in the EU still lies with the nation states in the Council of Ministers.

Why was the EEC a common market and not simply a Customs Union or free trade area (FTA)? Distinguishing between these three schemes provides the answer. An FTA abolishes customs duties and quotas between members; a Customs Union is the same as an FTA but also imposes a Common External Tariff (CET) on outsiders. A Customs Union was legal under GATT Article 24 providing the CET was no bigger than current duties and reduced to zero over time. Both FTAs and Customs Unions could be interdependent organisations. A common market was a Customs Union which also pursued common policies inside; accordingly a common market was an integrated supranational body simply because of these common policies.

Why did the Treaty of Rome 1957 establish an EEC with common policies in a common market and not just an FTA or Customs Union? The principal architect of the EEC, Pierre Uri, followed Friedrich List, the nineteenth-century German economist, in thinking that free trade in a technologically advanced era only made sense between countries whose industries were developed to the same extent. Simple free trade could not satisfy French national economic needs as much of French artisanal industry was internationally uncompetitive. Also, a free trade area would only cover trade in industrial goods not agriculture (which employed 28 per cent of the French labour force in 1955) nor would it accommodate France's colonies.

Moreover, simply opening frontiers to trade would be unfair as it would lead to distorted trade patterns as governments pursued different economic policies. Some heavily subsidised industrial exports, some had anti-monopoly laws, or imposed a heavy burden of social security costs on employers or followed deflationary policies. Free trade was considered insufficient as differences in national economic policies had to be dealt with. Consequently a common set of rules for a common market was devised so that member states would not 'play the same economic game by different rules'. This has always been the logic behind the Common Market's regulations on, for example, competition policy, the Common Agricultural Policy and the harmonisation of social security payments and benefits. Lynch shows that the French car industry's prices were much higher than her competitors due to higher wages and social charges (Lynch, 1993, p. 79). It was therefore considered essential to try to equalise social security costs (which in France could amount to as much as 40 per cent of the employers' wage costs) so that no 'unfair' burden was imposed on industries in a common market.

Similarly, there could be no simple free trade in arable, livestock and dairy products within a Customs Union because agricultural subsidies and protection varied so much between the six. Something else had to be devised – the French were insistent on the creation of a Common Agricultural Policy within the Treaty of Rome 1957, with common prices, protection and subsidies within 'Little Europe'.

The objective behind creating a common market was that it would lead to one large amalgamated economy of 170 million consumers at the end of a 12- to 15-year transition period. Six national economic systems would then, it was thought, be fused effectively into one domestic economy through common policies, common rules, the free movement of goods, labour and capital.

Pierre Uri and other architects of the Common Market 1955–57 expected that national responsibility for economic prosperity and full employment would be assumed by a supranational EEC, resulting in fiscal, monetary and even political union. In reality it has taken 40 years for the European Community to embark on a process leading perhaps to Economic and Monetary Union (EMU) by 1999 under the timetable established at the Maastricht Summit and under the Treaty on European Union 1992. However, back in 1970 EMU was supposed to be attained within a decade.

How did the move towards a common market and Euratom start? Monnet by 1955 had become enthusiastic about the collective commercial development of atomic energy by 'the Six', given the success of the ECSC. Joint European action on the nuclear front was an attractive prospect in the mid-1950s as it would reduce dependence on Middle East oil and American coal. Gas and oil extraction in the Sahara had not begun and North Sea natural gas off Holland had yet to be discovered. Nuclear power seemed to be the fuel of the future. Western Europe appeared short of energy resources at this time, a fact demonstrated vividly by the Arab oil embargo in the wake of the 1956 Suez crisis. The peaceful use of atomic energy became a matter of high priority with the cutting off of Europe's oil supplies. Collective co-operation in atomic energy made sense as the Six could pool their technical expertise and knowledge, and use Belgian uranium in the Congo, with Germany sharing the cost of building separators and reactors.

Jacques Beyen, the Dutch Foreign Minister, had proposed the formation of a common market in 1952 (combining it with the EDC/EPC schemes). He revived the idea in early 1955 in response to Mendès-France's proposed 'Franco-German economic committee' of December 1954, that was intended to bind the two economies more closely together (Lynch, 1993, pp. 75–6). Beyen could not allow Benelux to be excluded, as while there was some substance in Walter Lippman's colourful description in 1962 of the EEC as 'a bargain between French agriculture and German industry' the reality was more complex. In 1957 the Netherlands supplied more agricultural products to Germany than France, and imported more German vehicles and machinery than the French.

Initially the French Foreign Ministry was not keen on the idea of a common market and for many West European statesmen it seemed almost inconceivable that the French could ever be converted to anything approaching free trade. However, as we shall show, the French economic ministries came to regard a common market as the solution for France's economic predicaments. The reverse was true in Germany where the Foreign Ministry and Chancellor Adenauer were enthusiastic about the political benefits whereas the Economic Minister Ludwig Erhard was very much opposed to a common market, seeing harmonisation of social charges as a threat to German competitiveness (Milward, 1992, p. 213).

Consequently there were internal departmental arguments in both France and Germany over the merits of a common market, 1955–57, and also much hard bargaining between the six states over the terms of the Rome Treaties.

Following discussions between Monnet, Beyen and Spaak (Belgium's Foreign Minister 1954–57) both the idea for a common market and Euratom were to be formally proposed at the Messina Conference of the six foreign ministers in June 1955. Monnet and Spaak were much more positive about Euratom than a common market but Beyen was insistent that it was both or neither. The six foreign ministers were meeting in Sicily to appoint Rene Mayer as Monnet's successor as President of the ECSC's High Authority. This was because France was the only ECSC member that did not want Monnet to serve a second five-year term as ECSC's President. Monnet had effectively become persona non grata within French governing circles following a dispute with Mendès-France over the dilution of supranational controls in late 1954. Monnet, who really wanted to continue in the post, resigned and set up the 'Action Committee of all the Non-Communist Political Parties and Trade Unions of the Six', as a pressure group for further European integration.

Spaak and Beyen's paper on the dual proposal formed the basis of the conference communique to establish a common market and Euratom. Messina in 'Euro-mythology' is regarded as the starting point for '*la relance européenne*' after the EDC's collapse and the birthplace of the Common Market.

A small team was assembled under Spaak's chairmanship to study the schemes and draw up plans, including experts from the ECSC in Luxembourg such as Monnet's right-hand man, the imaginative French economist Pierre Uri. Another Frenchman, Robert Marjolin, resigned as Secretary-General of the OEEC to take part. The German team included Adenauer's mentor on foreign affairs, the Permanent Under-Secretary of Foreign Affairs, Professor Walter Hallstein. The British sent as their representative a Board of Trade official – Russell Bretherton, a former economics don at Wadham College, Oxford. He was initially briefed to try and steer the talks towards an OEEC free-trade area framework for West European commerce and trade. When this failed the UK became only an observer at the talks and finally left to try and undermine the proceedings (Young, 1989, p. 210). In May 1956 the Spaak Report (mainly written by Pierre Uri) was submitted to another

Foreign Ministers' conference in Venice and broadly approved. The same team was then consigned to the Château de Val Duchesse outside Brussels to draw up a Treaty. The Spaak Report emphasised the necessity of fusing separate national markets as 'the strength of a large market is its ability to reconcile mass production with the absence of monopoly'. It went on to argue that the

> advantages of a common market cannot be obtained . . . unless measures are taken to put an end to practices whereby competition between producers is distorted; and unless co-operation is established between the states to ensure monetary stability, economic expansion and social progress.

The Spaak Report's proposal for a common market went much further than Britain's simple aim of a free trade area. The whole process of establishing the EEC and Euratom took place extraordinarily quickly and, compared with the EDC episode, relatively painlessly. The Treaty of Rome was signed on 25 March 1957 and ratified by the six parliaments by July 1957.

Why did the six governments of 'Little Europe' sign what was essentially a commercial treaty, and their parliaments subsequently ratify it? The obvious reason was because it was the right thing to do. What they had decided to create proved to be a mutually beneficial political and economic framework for the continued expansion of trade, industrial and agricultural growth in Western Europe.

There was diplomatic pressure from the OEEC to reduce tariffs and quotas on intra-European trade and also move to full currency convertibility. The US pressed for yet another attempt at European unity. Although in 1954–55 the Foreign Offices of 'the Six' believed that French agricultural and industrial interests would never accept a common market, attitudes had and were changing in France because of economic circumstances. By 1957 France recognised that a common market in 'Little Europe' was the right commercial framework for French national economic and diplomatic objectives.

French experience in the ECSC revealed that anxiety over their supposed industrial inferiority and lack of competitiveness (because of a heavy social security bill) had been exaggerated. Also, since 1946 the French economy had been modernised under successive four-year reconstruction plans and the largest and most modern firms were becoming more export-minded. Exports were considered vital to continued growth and expansion. In a sense this modern export sector in France had the worst of both worlds as they were faced with competition from Volkswagen and Grundig in export markets while bearing the cost of measures intended to coddle artisanal old-fashioned businesses in France. The export sector had competition in the export markets but not at home where it could have revitalised antiquated French business. The dynamic export-orientated element of French industry was attracted to the EEC and had considerable influence with the French civil service. French Economic Ministries were eventually convinced that to complete the modernisation of French industry, the whole manufacturing sector, including protected artisanal industries, should receive shock therapy by being immersed in a competitive common market.

A common market also looked an increasingly attractive solution to the problems facing the French government with the Departments and Territories of Metropolitan France (Dom-Toms). Even before the Dutch proposed a common market in 1955 French officials in October 1954 were discussing the possibility of Germany investing in their Dom-Toms because France alone could no longer afford to. Moreover, the proposed full convertibility of currencies would end the main protection French goods enjoyed in the Franc Area of the Dom-Toms, and an OEEC agreement in 1954 to open up colonial trade to all members also threatened France's commercial monopoly of Dom-Toms' trade. Frances Lynch has shown that French goods cost 19 per cent more in the Dom-Toms and so cross-subsidised cheap French exports to the rest of the world. Algeria was a particularly big market, taking 21 per cent of French car exports in 1954 (Lynch, 1993, p. 71). Lynch showed French planners recognised that with the OEEC agreement ending France's monopoly of Dom-Tom commerce there could be advantages in linking the French Union's Dom-Toms with 'Little Europe'. By doing so France might gain the quid pro quo of Germany and the others' net contributions to French colonial investment in return for open markets.

This was indeed the case. The EEC's Overseas Devlopment Fund had $581.25m to invest between 1958–63. Both France and Germany contributed $200m each to this fund, yet France's African Dom-Toms received the bulk of the money, some $511.25m (Mahotière, 1961, p. 34).

The third reason for the French conversion towards a common market was that under the second Monnet Plan it was planned to increase agricultural output by 20 per cent (Lynch, 1993, pp. 75–6). France contained 47 per cent of 'Little Europe's' agricultural land and even in 1961 farming employed 20 per cent of the French workforce. French agriculture was under-mechanised so there was potential for a massive growth in production (an increase in output per man or per hectare), which would increase output well beyond the demands of the French

LEEDS COLLEGE OF BUILDING

market. Without secure markets this expansion could not proceed as it would only result in falling prices and farm incomes. The whole point of this French government plan was to raise the rural standard of living fairly quickly. In the mid-1950s West Germany imported a third of its food and, as Lynch has shown, France was negotiating to sell 2m tonnes of wheat per annum for three years to West Germany in 1954. However, Germany was insisting on full reciprocity, exporting goods to the same value that French quota restrictions currently excluded (a case of 'I'll eat your wheat if you drive my Volkswagens'). If France accepted the German demand for reciprocity, France would almost certainly have to extend it to countries like Switzerland and Britain, which up to then had imported French wheat without requiring reciprocity.

When Beyen proposed fresh talks about starting a common market in 1955 the consequences for France and particularly increased competition for French industry, were little different to what the Germans were demanding in return for buying French wheat (Lynch, 1993, p. 77). For French officials in the Economic Ministries concerned with planning, the Dom-Toms and agriculture, a common market began to look an attractive policy option in 1954–55. France's diverse national economic objectives might best be secured through an integrated common market framework rather than any other arrangement.

This again tends to confirm Milward's thesis that economic integration occurs when it is needed by nation states and when national policy objectives depended on links with West Germany. Only when attainment of national economic objectives hinged on a German connection then integration and supranational organisations (ECSC and EEC) followed.

Although the Common Market was a Dutch initiative the Treaty of Rome 1957 largely reflected French preoccupations. France was in a very strong bargaining position as no one wanted the French National Assembly to reject a second Treaty and without France nothing could happen. However, any rejection by France of the Common Market would have wrecked its policy of economic rapprochement and co-operation with Germany adopted in 1948–49. In contrast to the powerful French opposition to the EDC, strong political support was mobilised in favour of the EEC in France. Jean Monnet and his 'Action Committee' were prominent here. This was an organisation of political parties not individuals; the logic being that if the main political parties and trade unions could be won over to the idea of European economic integration, few governments could resist the pressure. A key conversion was that of Eric Ollenhauer and his German SPD party, which made it easier for French Prime Minister Guy Mollet's Socialist Party (the SFIO) to forget its schism over the EDC and accept the new EEC initiative, as it was backed by the other socialist parties of 'the Six'.

Also Maurice Fauré, in charge of European Affairs at the Quai d'Orsay and elected by a rural district, kept in close contact with French agricultural leaders during the negotiations. French agriculture's eventual conversion was of critical importance for French parliamentary acceptance of the Treaty – without it the Treaty would have failed. In July 1957, the French Assemblée Nationale voted by a comfortable majority – including all the socialist and most of the rural votes – to accept the Treaty of Rome. In the German Bundestag both the CDU and the SPD voted almost unanimously in favour.

Although for France the main reason for signing the Treaty of Rome was economic, a supranational common market would help guarantee the peace of Western Europe as the continued growth of trade and prosperity should enhance both its internal and external security. Moreover, a common market might provide a platform for the reassertion of French regional leadership in Western Europe.

In West Germany's case, however, the reason for agreeing to the Rome Treaties was largely political. Ludwig Erhard, West Germany's Economics Minister, strongly opposed a common market on economic grounds. He preferred a free trade area in which German industry would flourish. It was Konrad Adenauer who persuaded Erhard to acquiesce with the arrangements for a common market. Adenauer's main aim was to achieve a reconciliation between West Germany and its West European neighbours; France was crucial to this. Adenauer, just as with the ECSC and EDC previously, insisted on being an equal partner with equal status, and was determined to continue his west-orientated policy of embedding the Federal Republic in Western Europe.

Nevertheless, there was a great deal of hard bargaining particularly over the French demand for harmonisation of social security costs, which Erhard considered a threat to German manufacturing competitiveness (Milward, 1992, pp. 212–13). Erhard believed that Adenauer's foreign policy would impose at French insistence a crippling burden of additional security costs on the German economy. For example, France had a 40-hour week (compared to 45 hours in Germany), longer holidays and, in principle, equal pay for women. France insisted that the automatic timetable of tariff reductions at the end of the first stage was in fact conditional on progress in standardisation of such measures and costs. Negotiations eventually became deadlocked on 22 October 1956, only to be resolved at an Adenauer–Mollet meeting on 6 November. Between these two dates events in Hungary (where the USSR crushed a popular uprising against communism) and in Egypt where Anglo-French forces invaded, in collusion with Israel, made this Franco-German dispute about overtime pay look rather trivial. Adenauer and Mollet on 6 November swiftly resolved all outstanding disagreements delaying Treaty completion (Milward, 1992, pp. 214–15).

The old orthodox view of the significance of the Suez crisis was that it had a decisive effect on the French, propelling them into an agreement with Germany. To force the British to withdraw the Americans precipitated a sterling crisis. The pound sterling, unlike the French franc, was convertible to dollars and therefore vulnerable to American financial pressure. The US traded sterling for dollars, UK reserves fell by $50m and the UK was brought to heel by the Americans. The traditional view was that France therefore saw Britain as a weak unreliable partner, subservient to the Americans and therefore signed up with the Federal Republic of Germany instead. Milward's research shows that this view, though neat, was not fact. Both leaders, irrespective of British behaviour, had moved towards agreement prior to Suez. On 6 November, Adenauer and Mollet agreed so quickly they barely bothered to read the document (Milward, 1992, p. 215).

Although this smoothed the way for the EEC coming into existence, there were another four years of argument after 1958 over the CAP. The first moves were made at the Stresa Conference in 1958 and with the EEC Commission's proposals in 1960 to merge six different systems of agriculture into one common policy. Some states, like the Netherlands, had an expansive, aggressive policy; others, like Germany, were protective and defensive towards their agriculture (using direct subsidies to farmers, quotas and bilateral arrangements to insulate their small peasant farmers). The CAP, which France was insistent on and which involved years of argument between de Gaulle, Adenauer and Erhard, led to the abolition of all these protective measures in Germany and elsewhere. Instead there was to be a free exchange of agricultural goods combined with a uniform minimum level of prices and a guaranteed market (through storing and dumping of surpluses, exercising 'community preference', i.e. prioritising the purchase and guaranteeing a market for EEC produce and imposing big duties (agricultural levies) on competitive imports into the EEC). The CAP evolved into a highly regulated and protected market. If prices were not fixed according to sound economic criteria, enormous imbalances in production would arise. Cereal prices were vitally significant being a staple food and animal feedstuff, thereby affecting the prices indirectly of all animal products (milk, eggs, meat).

The price of corn was only agreed in 1964. Germany demanded a high price (as this was vital for their peasants' living standards) which meant an average price increase of 18 per cent in the EEC. In France it meant a 30 per cent price increase. France also had the greatest potential to increase production. From 1964 the guiding principles behind the CAP – high prices and a guaranteed market – could consequently only result in time in over production and 'structural surpluses' (Priebe, 1973, pp. 312–14).

Adenauer's motives for co-operating with a 'French-style' common market were basically political, yet the arguments over the precise arrangements were invariably economic. However, West Germany benefited enormously from both the Common Market and the CAP. West German GNP per head between 1958–72 grew by 178 per cent, in France by 185 per cent, in UK (who pulled out of the EEC process) by only 140 per cent, and in Italy by 180 per cent.

Was it the expectation of such growth that encouraged the Italian government to sign the Rome Treaties? In fact, in all six states in 1955–58 predictions of economic doom were as common as optimistic forecasts concerning the effect of a common market. In Italy, which had the highest tariff barrier in Western Europe, the fear was that its car and refrigerator industries would be destroyed by free market competition from Germany. In fact, Italy was extremely successful in selling cars and refrigerators in the EEC.

According to Federico Romero, Italy's main objective in the EEC was to encourage 'rational productive emigration'. They needed to export their unemployment, particularly from the underdeveloped south. Italy wanted and tried to win acceptance for the 'free circulation of labour' inside the EEC to complement the principle of a 'free movement of goods'. The government's main goal was an open European labour market to drain off Italy's massive unemployment (Romero, 1993, pp. 38–9). They failed to achieve this in 1957 because the other five members' priority was the antithesis of this: to safeguard jobs for their national work force. A 'common labour policy' and the free market for labour that Italy wanted conflicted with the other states' goals of controlling immigration and protecting domestic employment. Moreover, it would seem that the Italians made an error in 1955–57 in not negotiating an EEC 'community preference' for EEC labour. The growing demand for labour in the 1960s boom meant non-EEC Turkish and Portuguese migrants entered the EEC, particularly in Germany and Holland. There was no Treaty obligation to give priority to EEC migrants that would have benefited Italy (Romero, 1993, p. 54). Article 49 of the Rome Treaty made the free movement of labour an objective to be achieved in three stages by 1 July 1968 when work permits were abolished.

The regulations facilitating this were devised between 1961 and 1968. Regulation 15/61 allowed the free movement of labour only if there was no suitable worker available from the regular labour force of the other state. Nonetheless, it was thought that by late 1961 Germany had one million foreign workers in its farms and factories – the largest portion being Italian. Italy also needed EEC help with its economic development; the European Investment Bank and European Social Fund (ESF) were concessions to Italy. One of the first ESF schemes was the redeployment of 10,000 Italian workers to Germany and Holland to take up jobs in building, catering and industry. The ESF paid half the expense incurred by governments or employers' organisations to resettle or retrain workers; the ESF also helped provide lodgings and ensured they benefited from German and Dutch social security schemes (Mahotière, 1961, pp. 35–6).

Although Italy won these concessions from the EEC it failed in its ambitious objective of getting 'Little Europe' to share the burden of its unemployment in the late 1950s (Romero, 1993, p. 57).

Britain's refusal to join the EEC at the start is now seen as one of the biggest mistakes of post-war international statesmanship. Although there were previous occasions when the UK declined to take a lead or participate in supranational bodies, the major error was in 1955–56 when the Conservative government under Anthony Eden entered and then left the Spaak Committee's talks. The EEC only started to function in 1958, yet already by December 1960 the Conservative Prime Minister, Harold Macmillan, had changed his mind and decided to join a club whose rules Britain had not helped to write. Britain's two applications to join were then vetoed by de Gaulle in 1963 and 1967. De Gaulle held the key and he locked Britain out. Britain only entered the EEC in 1973 after de Gaulle had resigned as French President in 1969. It had taken Britain 13 years to become a member.

How could such a miscalculation have been made? What factors explain Britain's ineptitude? Traditional explanations invariably pointed to Britain's insularity. As an island and also a maritime power she combined a 'Little Englander' outlook with global responsibilities. Also, the old balance of power doctrine meant that Britain's instinctive reflex was to throw its weight against any new power bloc that emerged in Europe (Napoleon III, Hitler, Stalin – and now the EEC?). Moreover it is often argued that Britain's wartime experience, 1940–41, reinforced its faith in its own national sovereignty and parliamentary tradition. In contrast, 'the Six', who were defeated and occupied and then collaborated, embarked on economic integration. As a result a psychological gulf existed between countries like Britain, Sweden, Switzerland and 'the Six' simply because of their different experience of the war (Beddington-Behrens, 1966, p. 17).

Nevertheless, while there is truth in such observations we have to remember that Ernest Bevin (Foreign Minister 1945–51) encouraged European unity before 1948–49, as Chapter 3 showed. After 1949, with the US firmly committed to West Europe's defence, Britain reverted to a policy of 'limited liability' towards Europe, discouraged any initiative that might encourage the Americans to pull out and focused on its global problems.

Britain was still the third greatest global power in 1945 with 1.5 million men in its armed forces around the world. Atomic bomb tests in 1952 reinforced Britain's self-image as one of the Big Three globally and not as one of the Big Three in Europe. The reality though was that the UK could no longer afford its global role, having lost 25 per cent of its wealth in World War II (cf. 15 per cent in World War I). Defence spending equalled 28.5 per cent of total government expenditure in 1953, which meant very high tax rates (Churchill paid 19s. 6d. in the pound tax on the royalties from his war memoirs). Global defence commitments of 'UK World Power Inc. Ltd. Co.' were a big financial burden on an overloaded ailing economy, and the hundreds of thousands of men in the forces also strained the manpower budget as they were only consumers and not producing anything to sell. In retrospect, the UK's self image in the early 1950s was a delusion, she was a medium-ranked power not comparable to the US or USSR. Colonial and foreign affairs were given too high a priority by Britain's governing class. Considerable attention was devoted to closing down the Empire but scant thought was given to Britain's economic and political future without one. Both Eden, Prime Minister from 1955–56, and R.A. Butler (Chancellor) admitted they were 'bored by European issues' and Harold Macmillan, Foreign Secretary, failed to pay Europe sufficient attention. On 11 November 1955 it was the Economic Policy Committee, and not even the full Cabinet, that decided against joining the EEC – neither Eden nor Macmillan were present (Young, 1989, pp. 213, 217).

France prioritised Europe rather than its *vocation mondiale* from 1950 as it had to construct a framework safely to accommodate West Germany and provide access to its coal and markets. Britain was unable to make a similar volte face in policy until after the failures of Suez in 1956 and the last Four Power talks in Paris in 1960 (following this the two superpowers never asked Britain and France to their summit meetings again). These setbacks meant that in governing circles the painful reality of Britain's position as a declining power was indisputable and the policy changed. By then it was too late to join the EEC at its outset. Britain had 'missed the European bus' for three fundamental reasons: an absence of any forethought; a bad error of judgement in adopted policy; and a misplaced confidence and belief in the Commonwealth's commercial significance as an alternative to the EEC.

A key factor in Britain missing its opportunities in Europe was that no one gave it any serious thought at the Foreign Office between 1949–55. The Foreign Office was overwhelmed by problems and paperwork; the number of incoming papers in 1913 was 68,000 but by 1950 it was 630,000 (they doubled between 1939–50). When Eden became Foreign Secretary in 1951 he said 'the workload had killed Bevin, destroyed Morrison and now he understood why'. Eden was seriously ill within two years (Adamthwaite, 1988, p. 3). The British Foreign Office's conduct of foreign affairs traditionally followed the 'shopkeeper' approach (dealing with things as they turned up in a pragmatic fashion), not the more 'heroic' approach of framing realistic objectives and pursuing them rigorously at others' expense if necessary. The British tradition was bereft of vision, thought or any sense of direction. It was not just Eden who was responsible: successive Permanent Under-Secretaries who ran the Foreign Office admitted that they were 'permanently overtaken by events' and adopted a purely 'day to day approach' (Adamthwaite, 1988, p. 17).

Sir Ivone Kirkpatrick, in charge of the Foreign Office when Eden was Foreign Secretary 1951–55, said in his memoirs that there was 'little time to think, look ahead and make wise long term plans' (Kirkpatrick, 1959, p. 267) and he admitted that he had little time or interest in 'research, analysis or prolonged discussion'. This amounts to a systemic failure in foreign policy formation. Britain missed her chances as no one in the mid-1950s thought about where Britain should be or what would be in her best interests 10 or 15 years ahead. Churchill's general conception of Britain's foreign policy position (that Eden also endorsed) was that she lay at the centre of three interlocking circles of influence: with the US, the Commonwealth and Europe. Between 1949–61 Britain avoided too close a connection with Europe, not wanting to jeopardise the special relationship with the US (ironic given US policy towards European integration) or weaken Britain's connections with the Commonwealth. Prioritising these 'two circles of influence' was understandable in the late 1940s as Europe was poor, weak and discredited.

By the mid-1950s, however, Anglo-American relations were more often strained than special, commercial and military ties with the Commonwealth had weakened while Western Europe recovered quickly and continued to develop as the fastest growing market outside the US.

Nevertheless Foreign Office policy continued as before, determined to avoid any further loosening of ties with the US and the Commonwealth.

These two Foreign Office priorities were a major reason for the government's fateful decision in November 1955 to leave the Spaak Committee's negotiations on a common market. Originally, in June 1955, Britain was a full participant, represented by Russell Bretherton of the Board of Trade. He was briefed to try to steer the talks away from a common market to turning the OEEC into a free trade area. When he failed to do this the Foreign Office disengaged from the talks before Britain became associated with the final report. The Foreign Office tried to disrupt and divide 'the Six' by working on the tensions and differences of opinion between Adenauer and Erhard tempting them to abandon supranationalism for a free trade area. This failed but upset 'the Six' as it was seen as sabotage.

John Young's research in Cabinet, Foreign Office and Board of Trade papers revealed that while the Common Market was generally seen as being bad for British interests all the reports warned that if a common market formed Britain would have to join it, having had no say in its original structure, otherwise as a powerful economic bloc it would operate against Britain's interests. Sir Frank Lee of the Board of Trade even argued that the balance of advantage lay in joining the Common Market at the start (Young, 1989, pp. 206–12). However, the Cabinet decision not to join left Britain with a negative, inept and potentially dangerous policy of staying out while recognising that if a common market was established it would have to be in it! The vital moment of entering the Common Market at the start was missed in November 1955 when the rules were drawn up. British officials and ministers gambled that the Germans could be persuaded to join a free trade area, that the French would never accept a common market, and that 'the Six' had recently failed with the EDC.

The Foreign Office assumed that 'the Six' had federalist intentions and so misread the economic motives behind the Spaak Committee talks. The advice of Gladwyn Jebb, Britain's Ambassador in Paris, was that the Common Market would never happen.

Britain's miscalculation in 1955 appears extremely erroneous especially as officials realised already that the UK's power was declining, that Commonwealth trade was likely to fall and that if a common market suceeded it would harm Britain's interests, making membership essential (Young, 1989, p. 219). This decision, though wrong in retrospect, was not controversial at the time (a decision to enter would have surprised everyone including 'the Six'). Public opinion was not in favour of entry in 1955–56. However, apart from the Liberal Party this was still the case in

December 1960 when Macmillan changed his mind. So it does not absolve Eden's government (1955–56) for a failure in decision-making and leadership.

In May 1956, meeting in Venice, 'the Six' finally approved the Spaak Committee's reports and decided to press on with draft Treaties. When the UK realised that the EEC was likely to come about there was consternation in the Foreign Office. Other states such as Switzerland, Sweden and Portugal pressured Britain to mount a counter-initiative to the Common Market. Britain duly proposed talks with 'the Six' to convert the 16-state OEEC into a free trade zone. However 'the Six' refused talks until the Common Market was established.

Negotiations in the Intergovernmental Committee of the OEEC formed under the Chairmanship of Reginald Maudling, British Paymaster-General, were held in 1958 to discuss creating a wider free trade area for manufactured goods. However there was nothing in the idea that appealed to France. Agriculture would not be included and France had food surpluses to export. Also OEEC members would benefit from EEC tariff reductions while accepting none of the obligations under the Rome Treaties.

Olivier Wormser, Head of the Economic Department of the French Foreign Office, saw these negotiations as an ill-conceived device whereby Britain could have access to a tariff-lowering EEC market on easy terms. Wormser also suspected that Britain wished to wreck the EEC from within, having failed to sabotage it from without (Mahotière, 1961, p. 68). General de Gaulle, who had taken over as the French President, disliked the EEC but detested free trade, which had no compensating political advantage for France. Moreover he didn't want to risk France playing a subordinate role to Britain again, as in World War II, or see Britain challenge French leadership in Western Europe. On 14 November 1958 the General's new Foreign Minister, M. Couve de Murville, was instructed to issue a press statement rejecting the OEEC free trade area plan incorporating the EEC.

Following this French rebuff Britain embarked on 'Plan G', Whitehall's scheme for setting up a European Free Trade Area (EFTA), as a rival organisation to the EEC. The EFTA Treaty was signed in Stockholm on 20 November 1959 and came into force following ratification in May 1960. It established a headquarters of 80 staff in Geneva (compared with 3,000 for the EEC in Brussels). EFTA was made up of most of the OEEC states that had not joined the Common Market (Britain, Norway, Sweden, Denmark, Austria, Switzerland and Portugal). Newspaper headlines announced that Europe was now at 'sixes and sevens'. Greece, Turkey,

Spain and Ireland originally attempted to establish some special relationship with the EEC. Finland became an associate EFTA member in 1961 and Iceland joined EFTA in 1970.

EFTA aimed to reduce tariffs between members in stages at a similar rate to the EEC and free trade was completed in December 1966. EFTA undoubtedly benefited small states like Sweden and Switzerland with low tariffs as they gained access to the heavily protected big market of Britain. For Britain EFTA was a completely lopsided commercial arrangement. Britain provided 51 million of EFTA's population of 89 million. Britain was the only big market. EFTA countries took only 10 per cent of British exports in 1960 and were never going to be a substitute for the EEC. The market of 'the Six' was 170 million.

However, Britain never intended EFTA to be an end in itself. Plan G was to demonstrate that an FTA could operate and thereby persuade 'the Six' into an association with 'the seven' creating a big free trade Europe of the OEEC states. Reginald Maudling, now the President of the Board of Trade in the UK, tried to bring this about in 1960 and so prevent the permanent division of Western Europe into two rival economic blocs.

It was a complete failure. An EEC commission report written by Jean-François Deniau, a French Inspector of Finances, condemned the Maudling 'Pan-European' solution. It argued that free trade could only be effective if there was a common policy to ensure 'fair' competition, that agriculture must be included, a regional policy devised and a CET established. Maudling's plan was also condemned by the Americans. Mr Dillon from the US Treasury explained that whereas the EEC was acceptable to the US, the simple free trade plan was not, because it had no compensatory political benefits; both schemes were potentially harmful to US trade. The UK's policy on Europe was consequently in complete ruin.

By an impressive feat of incompetence British officials and ministers had succeeded in bringing about the very situation they were so anxious to avoid six years before: exclusion from the EEC with the prospect of a trade war, while Britain's NATO forces in Germany helped defend its commercial rival the EEC.

Although EFTA had only come into force in May 1960, Harold Macmillan, during Christmas 1960, decided to reverse his policy and make a bid to enter the EEC. This was finally announced to the House of Commons on 31 July 1961 after much surreptitious preparatory footwork in Europe, the Conservative Party, the Commonwealth and Britain. Why did this change in direction occur?

It had been recognised in 1955 that if the EEC came about Britain would have to be part of it. Having failed twice to gain access in 1958 and

1960 by trying to set up a large free trade zone Britain had no option but to actually join. The commercial success of the EEC made this an urgent matter. The EEC's productivity increased by 19 per cent between 1957–61, faster than the US or UK (at 13 and 12 per cent respectively). The GNP of 'the Six' increased by 27 per cent in real terms between 1957–61 (compared with 18 per cent in US and 14 per cent in UK). How much of this growth was due to the Common Market is hard to say. Their economies had been growing very rapidly before 1958, in fact industrial output in 'Little Europe' increased by over 90 per cent between 1950–60 compared to 39 per cent in the US and 29 per cent in Britain. Growth rates of individual EEC members varied greatly between 1958 and 1963, Italy's GNP rose by 59 per cent compared to Belgium's 15 per cent. Nevertheless, as Professor Walter Hallstein, the first President of the EEC Commission, remarked, 'It may be objected that these growth figures are no index of the success of the Common Market; but my reply would be that they certainly show that it has not failed.'

French fears of industrial competition in the EEC had given way to the enthusiastic exploitation of the benefits of a very large common market. French industry was helped considerably by de Gaulle's 17 per cent devaluation of the franc which gave them a competitive edge that ensured commercial success. This was important as it meant there was little recourse to the battery of safeguards and escape clauses built into the Rome Treaty at French insistence, that would otherwise have restricted the pace of development within the EEC. As a Belgian diplomat remarked: 'we are condemned to succeed'. Although supranational schemes were an anathema to General de Gaulle (French President 1958–69) who believed in the sanctity of the nation state and '*L'Europe des Patries*', he nevertheless agreed to honour French commitments to the Treaty of Rome. The early success of the EEC convinced de Gaulle that it could serve French political interests, with French leadership and ideas and a close alliance with West Germany laying the foundations of a new Europe. This would restore to France '*la grandeur*' after the pain of decolonisation and '*l'héroïsme de l'abandon*'. A 'Paris–Bonn Axis', with France riding the German horse, would ensure French regional leadership in Western Europe, restore French prominence politically and diplomatically and provide a sense of mission post-decolonisation.

The other two tenets of de Gaulle's foreign policy were linked to this, the development of '*la force de frappe*', an independent nuclear strike-force, and an unswerving hostility to American leadership. De Gaulle detested the passive acceptance of American protection that, in his view, reduced Europe to 'protectorate status'. De Gaulle's objective was to replace

America with France in German affections. Britain's problem in the 1960s was that de Gaulle knew that Britain would always side with the US in his struggle with America. Nevertheless US investment in the EEC increased by 81 per cent between 1956 and 1961, growing fastest in Germany and Italy. Between 1958 and 1961, 608 American firms established themselves in the EEC as opposed to 235 in the rest of Europe. Industrial agreements and mergers between firms in the EEC rose from 50 in June 1959 to 190 by February 1962. By July 1963 customs duties between EEC states had been reduced by 60 per cent from the 1957 level. Britain was faced with the CET which resulted in Dutch and German tariffs being higher than in 1957 and France's slightly lower. Britain had excluded itself from a dynamic Customs Union of 170 million. Even in 1971 although the average CET was about 8.5 per cent (and the UK tariff 10 per cent) for some products the EEC's protective duty was very high. Britain's commercial vehicles faced a 22 per cent duty, 18 per cent on organic chemicals, 16–18 per cent on plastics, 18 per cent on tractors and 14 per cent on diesel engines (HMSO, 1971, p. 21).

Macmillan reversed policy in 1960 because the reality was dawning that the Commonwealth was not an important market for the type of high quality goods in which Britain specialised. Newly decolonised states in Asia and Africa might have large populations but were underdeveloped and so provided a poor market for British exports. They were also often ill-disposed towards the old metropolitan power in the early years of independence. Canada, Australia and New Zealand were large, rich territories but their combined population was only 30 million. South Africa left the Commonwealth in May 1961 before it was expelled (following the Sharpeville massacre, March 1960). British exports to the Commonwealth fell from 47 per cent to 42 per cent of total UK exports 1950–60 and this trend was to continue. For example, in Australia (with a population of 10 million) manufactured imports from the UK accounted for 70 per cent of its total imports in 1954. By 1960 they were under 50 per cent. The Australian–Japanese Trade Agreement of July 1957 meant an increase in Japanese imports into Australia. Between 1950 and 1960 Britain's trade with the Sterling Area as a whole rose by only 9 per cent and other countries by 19 per cent, whereas the share of total UK exports going to the EEC rose from 14 per cent in 1958 to 21 per cent in 1964.

There had been a substantial deterioration in both Britain's international economic and political position between 1956 and 1961. Failure at Suez in 1956 confirmed that Britain was no longer a world power. The US began to see the EEC, and in particular Bonn, as a strong and dynamic ally. John F. Kennedy (US President 1961–63) relied less upon Britain as a mentor in foreign affairs. The failure of the Paris Four Power summit in 1960 which Macmillan had arranged shook him badly, as from then on the two superpowers only conducted bilateral talks.

Events had demonstrated Britain's inability politically and financially to sustain an independent role: the long-preferred two circles of influence – the Commonwealth and the 'special relationship' with the US – had lost credibility. Europe, in the shape of the EEC, was the last resort. Britain had nowhere else to go. The idea of joining the EEC was therefore not popular in Britain as it signified national failure.

Jean Monnet's famous remark was proved correct:

> There is one thing you British will never understand: an idea. And there is one thing you are supremely good at grasping: a hard fact. We will have to build Europe without you; but then you will come in and join us.

Over Christmas 1960, Macmillan was facing up to the hard facts. In spite of Britain's cavalier treatment of her EFTA partners, Denmark was relieved to learn of Britain's intention to join the EEC, and Ireland also announced its intention to apply. Sweden and Switzerland were not pleased.

From 1961–63 Britain pioneered negotiations for entry for Denmark, Ireland and Norway. Henri Spaak led the EEC's team of negotiators and Sir Pierson Dixon, Britain's Ambassador in Paris, Sir Eric Roll, former Economics Professor at Hull, and Edward Heath led the British side. Monnet wanted Macmillan to accept the Treaty of Rome and, once inside, ensure that Commonwealth interests were safeguarded. However, the Government could not appear to be abandoning the Commonwealth given that 'the Six' would not agree to the UK maintaining indefinite preferential trading links with the Commonwealth.

There was no alternative to negotiation over every conceivable tropical and temperate traded commodity. Zero duty on tea, cricket bats and polo sticks was easily agreed. There was a great deal of argument over Canadian tinned salmon, Australian canned fruit, Cypriot sultanas and – critically – New Zealand lamb and dairy exports. There were long, difficult all-night negotiating sessions on British agriculture. On 14 January 1963, in the midst of these negotiations, General de Gaulle called a press conference and unilaterally rejected Britain's application for membership. This shock announcement astounded the five other EEC states and the Commission. Macmillan though had been warned of this possibility by de Gaulle in 1962. Although Article 237 of the Treaty of Rome invited others to join, the irony was that Spaak (who was leading the negotiations) insisted in 1957 that Article 237 should allow any of the six states to block the entry of a new member. The original reason for this was that socialists were worried that some future right-wing majority on the Council of Ministers might admit fascist Spain and Portugal.

Why did General de Gaulle veto British entry? There is evidence that what de Gaulle wanted from Britain was an offer of nuclear partnership allowing the two countries to work together and so save France a fortune on defence research costs. De Gaulle was too proud to ask Macmillan directly for this and while the idea had also occurred to Macmillan, he never suggested it either. However, during the Brussels negotiations on British entry, Macmillan met Kennedy at Nassau and signed the Polaris deal which put Britain's nuclear force into a NATO grouping, and marked the end of Britain's fully independent nuclear deterrent.

De Gaulle was never consulted about this and took great exception to it. He considered that the Anglo-American special relationship operated to the detriment of France. He regarded Britain as America's 'Trojan Horse' in Europe (allowing greater US penetration of the Common Market) and feared that the EEC could be subsumed in a colossal Atlantic grouping under US control. Kennedy's Philadelphia Address on 4 July 1962 referred to a two-pillar Atlantic Partnership between the US and a United Europe. De Gaulle hated this conception and saw Britain, aligned with the US, as insufficiently European and so unsuited for EEC membership. De Gaulle wanted to shut Western Europe into a fortress, with France holding the key, a prospect that was unappealing to both the Benelux states and the European Commission.

French industry was averse to British entry to the EEC and a public opinion poll in January 1963 showed that 61 per cent of Frenchmen considered the Franco-German Treaty of 22 January 1963 desirable. When asked with which country France should have closest ties, 40 per cent said Germany and only 25 per cent said Britain. French public opinion had changed markedly in the ten years since the EDC collapsed. Furthermore, it was extremely doubtful that de Gaulle was prepared to share the leadership of Western Europe with the UK, or risk being subordinate to Britain, and Macmillan had said in 1961 that 'we can lead better from within'. De Gaulle avoided isolation despite his unilateral rejection of UK membership as he retained the support of Konrad Adenauer, the 87-year-old Chancellor of the FRG.

The Franco-German Treaty was negotiated from September 1962 and signed on 22 January 1963. For Adenauer reconciliation with France was of prime importance. The Treaty was a French attempt to constrain permanently the scope of West Germany's independent action; it stipulated regular consultations with France on all important questions of foreign policy and common interests in order to achieve as much 'similarly directed activity as possible'. The effect of this Treaty was largely nullified though in May 1963 when the Bundestag (the FRG's Parliament) ratified into law a preamble to the Treaty confirming its faith in the Western Alliance and the need to integrate the EEC and the Atlantic Alliance. West Germany refused to accept permanent French leadership at the expense of its relations with the US.

Ludwig Erhard, who succeeded Adenauer as Chancellor in 1963, did not share de Gaulle's views on Europe, was unimpressed by the '*force de frappe*' and regarded Germany's relations with the US as being most important. De Gaulle threatened to walk out of the EEC unless Germany agreed the Common Grain Price. This had to be settled before the GATT (Kennedy Round) of tariff-cutting negotiations started. Erhard was enthusiastic about the commercial prospects of this, wanting greater access to the US market for German manufacturers. In December 1964 the grain price was agreed. This was the first major decision taken in the EEC since the abrupt termination of the enlargement negotiations in January 1963.

Following this in 1965 the European Commission proposed a 'package' of measures concerning the financing of the Common Agricultural Policy and the whole EEC. It proposed that funds collected from both the levies on agricultural imports and the CETs should be used directly to finance the EEC in place of the direct contribution made by member states. Dutch concern over the need for democratic political control of EEC funds meant that the Treaty of Rome was to be amended to give the European Parliament budgetary powers. The EEC's President at the time, Professor Walter Hallstein, was a federalist and regarded the Commission as a proto-European government. If the Council of Ministers approved the Commission's proposal, the Commission and Parliament's powers would be strengthened at the expense of the Council. The proposed package angered de Gaulle, who was strongly opposed to any strengthening of parliamentary powers that threatened the power of member states. A state of deadlock existed at the Council meeting of 30 June 1965 and the French commenced their boycott of the EEC on 6 July, the 'empty chair' policy. For the next six months France did not attend Council meetings and no decisions could be taken on any major EEC issue. The French boycott was a blatant infringement of Article 5 of the Rome Treaty.

De Gaulle precipitated this crisis and boycott to stop the automatic introduction of majority voting on 1 January 1966. Previously, when the

EEC back in 1961 moved from Stage 1 to Stage 2 (under the Rome Treaty's timetable at the end of 1961) agreement was needed both on CAP and that Stage 1 had been completed. This required unanimous agreement which proved enormously difficult. Five minutes before the set deadline on 31 December 1961 the Ministers had to 'stop the clock' at 11.55 p.m. and carried on negotiating until they agreed on 13 January 1962. However, the transition by 31 December 1965 from Stage 2 to Stage 3 of the Rome Treaty was to be an entirely automatic process that required no vote. In the third stage 'qualified majority voting' was to be introduced into the Council of Ministers. France, Germany and Italy were to have four votes, Belgium and Netherlands two, and Luxembourg one. A two-thirds majority, 12 out of 17 votes, would be needed for Commission proposals to succeed. This would mean a big country could only stop a proposal if it was supported by another country (other than Luxembourg). It was this that de Gaulle intended to stop.

De Gaulle's heavy-handed treatment of the EEC and the other five member states by a boycott that paralysed the Community from mid-1965 to early 1966, was a direct challenge to the institutional machinery of the 1957 Treaty. It ended in January 1966 with the 'Luxembourg Compromise'. The original Commission 'package' of proposed reforms was shelved. Neither France nor the other five states would change their position on majority voting so they agreed to disagree over the French insistence on a veto where 'vital national interests' were at stake. This compromise simply postponed a resolution of the issue. Margaret Thatcher (British Prime Minister 1979–90) tried unsuccessfully during the Falklands crisis to exercise the veto against a majority vote agreeing new farm prices in 1982. Under French pressure the EEC argued it was not applicable and refused to allow Britain to invoke the Luxembourg proceedings in this case. Higher farm prices appeared to be the *quid pro quo* for EEC support of Britain against Argentina. De Gaulle's action in 1965–66 had nevertheless resulted in unanimity becoming normal practice in EEC decision-making for the next 15 years.

In addition to retaining its veto, France had ten complaints about the Commission that required resolution – all were intended to clip its wings and reduce it to a functional executive body. The 'striped pants clause' was designed to curb the Commission President's ceremonial prerogative in receiving Ambassadors' credentials from diplomatic missions to the EEC. The result of such complaints and the compromise was that in future the Commission, having been intimidated, would be more restrained and less ambitious in its proposals. The French had won their point. De Gaulle had showed that if he did not get his way the Community's business could be stopped, which effectively meant that the EEC had to operate within parameters set by France. It also meant that power within the EEC did not ultimately lie with the Council of Ministers (and member governments) but with any strong, single government.

In 1967 Harold Wilson (Labour Prime Minister 1963–67) reapplied for membership without insisting on all the special treatment and safeguards for the Commonwealth that Macmillan had. In November 1967 a balance of payments crisis led to the pound being devalued. This provided de Gaulle with an excuse to oppose opening negotiations, arguing that Britain should solve her economic difficulties first. For a second time de Gaulle unilaterally rejected British membership without consulting her partners. The Commission and the other five states refused to accept this French diktat and proposed alternative ways to involve Britain in the WEU to discuss the development of a common foreign policy. This precipitated the temporary withdrawal by France from the WEU.

For France's five partners British membership of the EEC became crucial in the 1960s as Gaullist France excluded Britain in order to assert its hegemony. French obstruction to enlargement and development within the EEC, and her apparent indifference to isolation, only ceased with de Gaulle's resignation as President of France in April 1969. De Gaulle's brutal handling of the EEC was designed to extract the maximum economic benefit for France while using it as a vehicle to advance his own policies in Europe, with France – not the supranational EEC – as regional leader. Moreover, de Gaulle both demonstrated and ensured that the nation state remained dominant, retaining full economic and political control (in everything except trade and agriculture). This effectively destroyed the theory formulated by E.B. Haas (1958) and current in the 1960s, that an automatic spillover from successful economic to political integration would occur.

De Gaulle's successor as President, Georges Pompidou (1969–74) at his first Press Conference on 10 July 1969, switched policy and said he had no objection to British membership. In December 1969 on Pompidou's initiative an EEC heads of state summit was held at The Hague where a package was agreed to complete, deepen and enlarge the EEC. The final transition arrangements, as laid down in the Rome Treaty, were completed 18 months early. Full operation of the Customs Union was scheduled for 31 December 1969. The arrangements (shelved three years before) for financing the CAP were agreed and for direct funding of the EEC from its 'own resources' (revenue from agricultural import levies and

a proportion of VAT payments) rather than from states' annual 'membership fee'.

They also agreed to try and revitalise Euratom, which unlike the EEC
had not been a success. In the mid-1950s uranium was thought to be
scarce and so needed to be shared whereas it proved to be quite abundant.
Euratom failed too because de Gaulle's government opposed it and
although it had spent a lot on research and development (R&D) it had no
strategy for exploiting the products developed.

In anticipating enlargement with Britain's membership a European
Regional Development Fund was to be formed and the Lomé Convention
widened, covering EEC trade and aid relations with ex-colonies. Apart
from agreeing to start negotiations on enlargement with Britain, Norway,
Ireland and Denmark, The Hague summit also commissioned the
Werner Committee to report in 1970 on establishing a Monetary Union
by 1980.

Why did Pompidou change course and agree to Britain's entry? By
1969 France was uneasy about the economic and increasingly political
strength of West Germany and alarmed by its 'Ostpolitik' (Eastern Policy).
Britain's membership would be a counterweight to growing German
influence in the EEC. The development of *détente* between the superpowers from the mid-1960s (rather than Cold War rivalry and an arms
race) following the Cuban missile crisis of 1962 enabled West Germany to
embark on its Ostpolitik: trying to improve relations and the atmosphere
with Eastern Europe. After the Soviet Union crushed the Czechoslava-
kian democratisation process under Alexander Dubček (1968–69) – 'the
Prague spring' – West Germany's Ostpolitik continued but on Soviet
terms. West Germany had to pay a political price, recognise East
Germany, the 1945 borders, and compensate victims of the Nazis in
Eastern Europe. Willy Brandt's (Chancellor 1969–74) inaugural speech
on 28 October 1969 recognised East Germany as a separate state –
reversing 20 years of policy – and referred to Germany as 'one nation, two
states'. The following August 1970 West Germany signed with the USSR
the Treaty of Moscow, and in December 1970 the Treaty of Warsaw with
Poland.

West Germany's NATO and EEC partners in Western Europe had
misgivings about these developments and France was surprised at West
Germany embarking on an independent diplomatic initiative eastwards
when it had previously pursued a purely western-orientated policy. West
Germany, hitherto an 'economic giant but political pygmy', was now
using its economic strength as a political lever with Eastern Europe
(through trade agreements). Ostpolitik raised new fears of West Germany

being 'Finlandised' (having to remain permanently friendly to the USSR) or of having agreed a new 'Rapallo Treaty', signed by the USSR and Germany in 1922 pledging closer co-operation and establishing better relations that was both a challenge and a warning to France and Britain at the time.

Such fears were soon shown to be groundless. In fact Willy Brandt only felt sufficiently secure to pursue Ostpolitik because West Germany was so firmly embedded in the Western framework of the EEC and NATO. Nevertheless, Pompidou's response in 1969 was to bring Britain into the EEC to counterbalance West German influence. Twenty years earlier, in 1949, the emergence of a West German state had meant a complete change in French policy towards Germany (see Chapters 3 and 4) with the start of a Franco-German economic alliance. In 1989 the collapse of the Berlin Wall (9 November 1989) and the imminent prospect of German reunification meant that François Mitterrand (French President 1981–95) contemplated a closer Anglo-French co-operation with Margaret Thatcher. Both were uncomfortable about a rapidly reunified Germany. Mitterand apparently told Thatcher at the Strasbourg European Council 1989 'that at moments of great danger in the past France had always established special relations with Britain and he felt that such a time had come again' (Thatcher, 1993, p. 796). However, Mitterand was finally unwilling to abandon 40 years of close Franco-German co-operation. Instead, following German reunification and the complete collapse of Soviet power in Eastern Europe, the Treaty on European Union was agreed at the Maastricht European Council in December 1991. The French dash to European Union in the autumn of 1991 was intended to curb German power, to tie a united big Germany down in European Union and try and stop Germany translating its economic and financial power into political dominance. Helmut Kohl (Chancellor West Germany 1982–90 and Germany 1990– ) agreed to Maastricht's 'three pillars' of Economic and Monetary Union; co-ordination of foreign and security policy; and co-operation over 'justice and home affairs'. Kohl wished to stabilise his western relations to reassure EEC partners following reunification by portraying it as 'German unity in European Union'.

Whenever French anxieties have been raised over the 'German question' circa 1949, 1969 and 1989, the response was either to launch initiatives for further integration, develop closer relations with Britain or both.

EEC enlargement negotiations with Ireland, Norway, Denmark and Britain started in June 1970. Britain and the EEC had agreed the terms by

June 1971. Britain's tariffs were to be eliminated in five stages of 20 per cent reductions, the last reduction being in July 1977. This meant a four-and-a-half-year transition period to full membership. Britain was in a weak bargaining position. Edward Heath's Conservative Government (1970–74) was in no position to refuse the terms of entry. Britain had nowhere else to go.

Britain, Denmark and Ireland joined the Common Market in January 1973, 15 years after its establishment. (Norway withdrew its application following a referendum in 1972.) How did exclusion from the EEC affect the Danish and British economies? Denmark was a big supplier of meat to Germany in the 1950s. However, the community preference rule meant that much of this market was lost once the CAP was established. Danish exports to the FRG in 1972 were 75 per cent of their 1962 value while the value of Dutch exports had increased fourfold and French fivefold (Milward, 1992, p. 315). Between 1958–71 the growth of output in the EEC was 98 per cent, in Britain it was only 43 per cent. Britain was bottom of the OECD growth league in the 1960s and 1970s. The EEC growth rate was 5.4 per cent, Britain's was 2.8 per cent at best. The compounded effect over ten years was to raise the EEC standard of living (allowing for population changes) by 74 per cent compared to Britain's 31 per cent. Whereas in 1960 Britain had a standard of living higher than any EEC state, by 1970 it was lower than all EEC states except Italy (*Economist*, 14 August 1971). By 1980 Britain's standard of living had slipped below Italy's.

Although not the only cause of Britain's malaise in the 1960s, being outside the largest fastest-growing European market was a major factor. British manufacturers treated Europe in the 1950s as of secondary importance, preferring to focus on less competitive soft markets. The result was that manufacturers of consumer durables avoided competition in Europe with Italian, German and French producers. British firms, through avoiding competition, became less competitive, as they were not driven to improve design, raise productivity, undertake technological innovation and investment to the same extent as European firms. Between 1959–69 in the EEC 24 per cent of GNP was invested, in the UK it was 17 per cent. Moreover, within the Common Market, if a country's consumption of manufactures fell its manufacturers' output need not fall, as it might compensate by selling more to the rest of the EEC's Common Market (Milward, 1992, pp. 419–22). Britain could not do this and was faced with recurrent balance of payments crises and 'stop-go' policies.

By 1970 Britain was the only major car market where there had been no net growth since 1963 and car sales in 1970 were substantially below

1964. In 1969 West Germany's new car registrations were double Britain's. Both British manufacturers and the government in the 1950s had ignored the fact that Europe was the only big market in the world economy which bought the small and medium-sized cars that Britain manufactured. Membership of the EEC would have provided British car makers and other manufacturers with the security of permanent access to a market of 230 million. The Commonwealth and American markets did not offer this. Import surcharges on British car exports were imposed (e.g. Canada 1960, US 1971) whenever an importer was in economic difficulties. Australia adopted import substitution policies to encourage its own car assembly plants. British cars faced a 35 per cent imperial preference duty (other states 45 per cent) but component parts for assembly in Australia only had a 7 per cent duty to encourage foreign car makers to manufacture in Australia. General Motors and the British Motor Corporation did so, which hit British car exports again (Barber and Reed, 1973, p. 276).

By the late 1960s Ford UK and British Leyland both turned to the European market as Britain had become the smallest and most stagnant domestic market of any major car producer. From 1967 Ford integrated its European car making operations (making, for example, automatic transmissions at its Bordeaux plant). Ford also concentrated investment in Germany, rather than Britain, in order to supply the expansive German and EEC market. The British government's 1971 White Paper on *The UK and the European Communities*, by stating the advantages of membership, implicitly acknowledged the disadvantages of remaining outside the EEC for 15 years. It emphasised the benefits of a market of 300 million to spread R&D costs across bigger production runs, achieve greater economies of scale and specialisation. In the late 1960s Italian producers of refrigerators, Zanussi and Ignis, considered their optimal plant size, given the Common Market, was to make 800,000 p. a. while UK producers thought in terms of plants for 200,000 p. a. Italian machines, therefore, because of economies of scale, cost 15 per cent less to make. In 1966 three big independent UK companies were making computers – Elliott-Automation, International Computers and Tabulators (ICT) and English Electric – and were subject to intense US competition (they had 40 per cent of the UK market). In Europe the US had 89 per cent of the market. The UK's computer industry, unlike the United States', was thus handicapped by its restricted domestic market and was unable to meet the enormous development costs. The danger in the 1960s was that the whole UK and European computer market might fall into US hands (Beddington-Behrens, 1966, pp. 55–6).

Bringing UK high-technology industry into the EEC might have enabled Western Europe to compete more effectively against the American and Japanese electronics, jet aircraft and aero-engine industries. Both Britain and the EEC were afraid of American predominance in advanced technology industries in the late 1960s and early 1970s.

What effect did enlargement have on the EEC? It was beneficial economically as Britain, being a mature industrial economy, would be a net contributor to the EEC's budget. Britain imported 70 per cent of its food and had only 3 per cent of its labour force in agriculture – once inside the EEC, CAP preference rules meant Britain's 58 million consumers would be a big market gain for the EEC's farmers. Ireland and Denmark had small populations and were easily absorbed.

Enlargement from six to nine did make agreement in the Council of Ministers more difficult, given the need for unanimity following the Luxembourg Compromise. The EEC has been described as being in the 'doldrums' from the mid-1960s to the early 1980s (Pinder, 1983, p. 30) because there were few new initiatives and no further successful integration. Although the objective of EMU was inspired by recurrent international monetary crises and financial turbulence (in 1967 sterling's devaluation; in 1968 the dollar, gold and French franc crises), the breakdown of the Bretton Woods system of fixed exchange rates between 1971–73 and the oil price shock of 1973–74 resulted in EEC member states pursuing different monetary and foreign exchange policies rather than attempting to co-ordinate them as the EEC Commission wanted. The Werner Report's (1970) aim of creating a common currency by 1980 had been wrecked by 1973. All six member states were resistant to any transfer of control of economic or monetary policy to a supranational body.

The year 1973 marked the end of the 'long post-war boom', 1945–73, the break-up of the international monetary system based on fixed exchange rates, and the Yom Kippur war in the Middle East. This war resulted in an energy crisis, with a massive oil price increase from $2 per barrel mid-1973 to $10 in 1974 and $12 in 1975. The effect was worldwide economic recession, unemployment and inflation. The combination of inflation and stagnation ('stagflation') had several implications for the EEC in the 1970s. It challenged governments' policies and techniques for managing their economies. Orthodox Keynesian demand management, spending one's way out of unemployment and recession, would not work but simply cause more inflation and so worsen the problem. With such uncertainty the nine EEC states were not prepared to risk experimentation with EMU, which required the transfer of economic and monetary instruments from national to supranational control, when faced with balance of payments crises and inflation.

Instead in 1973 there was an agreement to float EEC currencies against the dollar and try to keep the six currencies' fluctuations between each other to a small margin. This arrangement was known as 'the snake in the tunnel'. Italy, Ireland and the UK did not join and France left in 1974 (in order to devalue), rejoined in 1975 only to leave again in 1976. In 1978 at the Bremen Summit, following EEC President Roy Jenkins' initiative of 1977, the European Monetary System (EMS) with an Exchange Rate Mechanism (ERM) replaced 'the snake in the tunnel'. It was felt that the worst effects of 1973–74 were now over. The EMS should provide a zone of monetary stability to benefit community trade. (Britain stayed out of the ERM at the time.) In 1979 another doubling of the oil price by OPEC meant that completion of the EMS originally scheduled for March 1981 (including a European Monetary Fund with central bank powers) was abandoned at the Luxembourg European Council meeting in April 1980. However, irrespective of the role of OPEC and oil prices in wrecking attempts at EMU and EMS, to have been successful would have meant a commitment to harmonise national economic and monetary policies. There was no sign of such policy convergence before 1984 as EEC members had different economic priorities: Germany to reduce inflation, France and Italy to reduce unemployment (Donges, 1981, pp. 20–4).

Another failure of EEC states to act together, with a community response, was during the 1973 oil crisis itself. The EEC did nothing to help defend Holland, a member state, when subjected to an Arab oil embargo (because it was considered pro-Israeli). Instead EEC members, notably France and Britain, moved quickly to make bilateral deals for oil with Arab states in the Gulf, in order to safeguard their own national oil supplies. The major oil companies helped Holland more than the EEC through supplying them by the clandestine diversion of oil shipments. The energy crisis revealed the inability of the EEC to act collectively as a 'community' with a common strategy towards OPEC's oil price increases 1973–75 and a shameful unwillingness to defend the Dutch and so jeopardise Anglo-Arab and Franco-Arab relations. The EEC looked like a community where economic integration and co-operation worked well in the commercially buoyant 1950s and 1960s but as soon as economic conditions got rough in the 1970s it was every member for itself.

The worst effect of the 1970s recession was that it threatened the whole operational success and integrity of a single common market by the growth of a new protectionism between member states and by the EEC with non-members. During the 1970s most EEC governments resorted to subsidising ailing industries during the recession. Such 'state aids' distorted competition in the Common Market but were justified by national governments to the EEC Commission on policy grounds (regional, employment or industrial restructuring). In 1975 the British government got the EEC Commission's reluctant agreement to a £1,500m rescue plan for British Leyland.

However the main problems were protectionist devices known as non-tariff barriers (NTBs) that proliferated in the 1970s. Member governments' different regulations concerning safety, public health, environmental protection were used as NTBs. A single market, for instance, in gas central heating boilers and cars was breaking up through the enforcement of different national safety regulations (e.g. Italy specified laminated car windscreens, Germany toughened glass). The EEC Commission attempted to harmonise such regulations into common EEC directives. In 1977 common EEC standards for cars were set. Harmonising different national specifications was a slow process – on average only seven directives were negotiated per year.

The EEC as a whole became more selectively protectionist in the 1970s, notably in protecting EEC textile and shoe industries from Third World competition by, for example, the Multifibre Agreement in 1974 (renewed in 1978 and 1981). The EEC also organised crisis cartels to help entire manufacturing sectors in distress, like the steel restructuring programme of 1977 reinforced by compulsory price and production controls in 1980 under the Treaty of Paris, Article 58. Only Ireland and West Germany did not use 'voluntary export restraints' to limit the number of imported Japanese cars. This encouraged the Japanese to build 'screwdriver' and then manufacturing plants in the EEC, mostly in Britain.

Britain's problem in 1973 was that she joined at the end of the long boom and had to adjust to the EEC and the heavy costs of membership at a difficult time. In February 1974 a new Labour government tried to negotiate 'new and fairer methods of financing the budget'. The UK Treasury estimated that while Britain would pay 24 per cent of the Community budget by 1980 its share of community GNP would be 14 per cent. At the Dublin Summit in March 1975 all they achieved was a 'budget correcting mechanism' which provided for a refund (of up to 3 per cent of the budget) if budget contributions were significantly beyond Britain's share of EEC GNP. In April 1975 a Commission Report on EMU written by Robert Marjolin (ex Vice-President of the EEC) reported on its complete failure. This helped both the Labour government in its negotiations in 1974–75, and also the pro-EEC lobby win a 2:1 majority in favour in Britain's referendum on EEC membership in June 1975, as it meant little prospect of further costly supranationalism (only in the Shetlands and Western Isles were there majorities against).

At the Fontainebleau Summit of June 1984 Margaret Thatcher eventually achieved 'financial justice' with a 50 per cent rebate reducing Britain's contribution from £1,000m to £500m p. a. The issue of Britain's 'budgetary imbalance' (as the EEC called it) and the connected rising cost of the CAP were both most time-consuming for the Council and represented the major preoccupation of the EEC between 1980–84. This cleared the way for further developments leading to the Single European Act (SEA) 1986 and the Iberian enlargement.

The key motive behind the Single European Act was to rescue the dynamic benefits of one large single market for European industry and commerce. The result of neoprotectionism in the 1970s was that the EEC had become less dynamic. The EEC was growing more slowly than Japan and the newly industrialised countries (NICs) of the Pacific Rim (S. Korea, Taiwan, Hong Kong, Singapore). The EEC seemed, at least compared to these 'Asian Tigers', to be suffering from 'eurosclerosis', and the danger was that its industries might be 'rolled over' by competitive Japanese and American transnational corporations. The tendency of some EEC states (France and Italy especially) to select and protect leading firms as 'national champions', feather-bedding them through public contracts meant that these companies focused on their domestic market, thus eroding the EEC's large Common Market. By the late 1970s and early 1980s more economists, government officials, and politicians recognised that to compete with Japan, the US and NICs, European companies needed to be globally competitive and treat the EEC as their 'home base'.

The European Council Meeting in Milan, June 1985, considered the EEC Commission's White Paper 'Completing the Single Market' and decided under Article 236 of the Treaty of Rome (1957) to convene a conference to consider a Treaty amendment. The result was the SEA signed 17 February 1986. Lord Cockfield, the Commissioner responsible for the internal market, was inspired in his White Paper by the Court of Justice's '*cassis de Dijon*' ruling of 1979 (a drink excluded from Germany on grounds that its alcoholic content was too high for wine but too low for spirits). The ruling introduced the new principle of 'mutual recognition' of national specifications so that 'legal manufacture meant legal circulation' throughout the EEC (if it was considered safe for Frenchmen to drink it was safe for Germans or anyone else in the EEC). Lord Cockfield and EEC President Jacques Delors aimed to develop this principle (that bypassed much of the need to harmonise regulations and standards for every product) and create a single internal market by '1992' with free movement of goods, people, services and capital. The 1985 White Paper listed 300 items that required resolution to complete the single market, including wholesale eradication of NTBs whether technical, physical or fiscal. It meant dispensing with most customs' formalities and reducing the costs of frontier delays for lorries; harmonising VAT rates; opening up public procurement through state contracts to EC competition.

While the SEA did introduce procedural changes for political co-operation and the co-ordination of foreign policy and a slight enhancement of the European Parliament's role and looked ahead towards creating an EMU, the main constitutional change was to extend qualified majority voting (QMV) over all internal market legislation. This change meant that for the first time, under the SEA 1986, all 'harmonisation' agreements were made by QMV, not unanimity. For a measure to pass into EC law required eight of the 12 states or 54 out of 77 votes. Harmonisation of regulations (on, for example, EC car exhaust emissions) became a quicker process and over 90 per cent of the 1985 White Paper's '1992' agenda was achieved by that date.

The other reason for introducing QMV was to avoid complete deadlock in EC decision-making if an enlarged EC of 12, including Spain and Portugal, had to achieve unanimity.

Spain and Portugal joined the EC in 1986 after eight years of negotiations (1978–86). Greece had joined in 1981 (following six years of negotiations). Applications for membership followed their return to democracy after years of dictatorship. Why did it take so long to negotiate Spanish entry? It proved much harder for the EEC to absorb a big, less-developed agricultural state because of the CAP, which provided free access to the European market at guaranteed prices. Spain would increase the EC's population by 20 per cent but GDP by only 10 per cent. Spain had surpluses in olive oil and citrus fruit to add to the EC's surplus. When Spain applied to join in 1977 the EEC budget was already under strain: the CAP took 80 per cent of the budget, whereas both Regional Aid and the Social Fund together accounted for 8 per cent. Spain's admission might wreck the EEC's budgetary and CAP arrangements unless reforms were made to both as Spain would also draw on Regional Development Funds. In 1984 a start was made to limit the upward growth of agricultural expenditure in the CAP through production quotas. By 1992 60 per cent of the EU budget was spent on the CAP and 28 per cent on Regional Aid.

Spain also had a huge fishing fleet – 50 per cent of the size of the total EEC fleet in 1980. Fishing was a highly sensitive matter in the EEC (of the

302 boats caught fishing illegally in EC waters in 1983–84, only five were not Spanish). The Common Fisheries Policy dating from 1971 required revision prior to Spanish entry. A new policy was agreed in 1983. Spain proved difficult to include in the EEC because of the sensitivity of existing members for their own national interests (whether fishing; citrus fruit and olive oil producers; the dispute with Britain over Gibraltar; or competition from Spain's steel and textile industries).

Absorbing a small agricultural state like Greece in 1981 was not too problematic: it only added 7 per cent to the EEC budget. Yet any future absorption of Poland's population of 35 million with 8.5 million farmers into current CAP arrangements and the EU would, it is estimated, increase the EU budget by 20 per cent. Turkey (population 52 million), an associate since 1963 with an application for full membership turned down in 1989, signed a Customs Union agreement with the EU on 5 March 1992. This excludes agriculture, which employs 55 per cent of Turkey's labour force.

Ex-Eastern Bloc economies and Turkey look to the EU's relative political and economic stability as a secure haven from Eastern Europe and the turmoil of Central Asia.

The 'Arctic–Alpine' enlargements of Finland (population 5 million), Sweden (population 8 million) and Austria (population 8 million) in January 1995 were easily absorbed as small rich economies that will be net contributors of £2.4bn to the EU's budget by the year 2000, and so eventually help fund the EU's enlargement to Central Europe.

Why do these states want to join the EU? Not, it appears, because they wish to see a federal Europe but because their neutrality was no longer a bar to membership with the end of the Cold War. Also, although they already had free access to the EU market (through the old EFTA states and EU creating the European Economic Area (EEA) 1993), they still wanted to become full members. The reason was that all their goods and products were subject to EC laws, regulations, standards and European Court of Justice rulings inside the EEA. The Arctic–Alpine EEA members did have a consultative role on new EC laws but no vote. Full EU membership would mean participation in decisions affecting their products, and so protect their national economic interests.

The other associated attraction of full EU membership for small states is that they have a disproportionate voting power and influence in the Council of Ministers. Both Austria and Sweden, with populations of 8 million, each have four votes; Germany, with a population of 80 million, has ten votes under current arrangements. (These conventions date back to 1957 and favoured the small states of 'the Six'.)

For the EU's neighbouring non-members, being outside the EU club and single market nevertheless means conforming to EU standards, regulations and laws. This is necessary both for any exports into the EU and because of the eventual requirements of 'acquis communitaire', if they were ever to join the EU club. So EU membership meant states were better able to protect their national economic interests inside, and participate in making decisions which would still have affected them even if they had remained outside. For small states, membership accorded them a disporportionate political weight to their population size in decisions.

Even though the Norwegian and Swiss electorates in 1994 and 1992 respectively rejected closer connections with 'the twelve', their governments and main political parties all favoured membership. This is not surprising given that the EU's single market now has 348 million people (cf. 259m in the US and 125m in Japan) and the EU accounts for 40 per cent of world trade.

# Epilogue

Economic integration under the treaties of Paris and Rome established a community system of nation states whose formative origins date back to the 1940s, emerging in the 1950s and developing under the Rome Treaty's timetable through the 1960s. In the 1970s the concept of a common market was threatened by the growth of new protectionism within it in response to economic recession and financial turbulence. The 1980s saw the restoration and extension of the Common Market through the Single European Act 1986 and the creation of the single market by 1992.

European integration was intended to serve the economic and commercial interests of nation states; decision-making was only pooled in a supranational organisation when those interests depended on links with Germany. The integrated arrangements of a common market proved a successful framework for otherwise independent and influential nation states to protect their economic security between members inside the EEC and from non-members outside.

As has been shown, part of the reason for the supranational ECSC 1951 and the 'three pillars' of the Treaty on European Union 1992 was the need to reformulate a solution to the German question. The two big questions facing Europe might not change but the solutions do. The collapse of Soviet power in Central Europe during 1989–91 and the reunification of the two German states has meant a further attempt at integration within the community system to embed big Germany into a European Union; the solution for East European states was membership of the EU (promised to Poland, Hungary and the Czech and Slovak republics) and preferably NATO too.

Nevertheless, to date only economic integration has really proved successful since the process commenced in 1950 (*vide post* EDC/EPC collapse and the Euratom flop). Efforts to co-ordinate other policies – such as the 1992 EU Treaty's agreements for co-operation over crime, justice and immigration and most notably since the 1970s in foreign affairs – have been kept outside the remit of the Rome Treaty's integrated framework. A common collective response by EC member states to international crises has understandably proved difficult to achieve given the divergent legacy of their global interests and experience. For example, in the Falklands crisis of 1982, Italy and Ireland declined to join the EEC sanctions imposed on Argentina; in the Yugoslavia crisis of 1991 Germany was at odds with the rest of the EC as Germany insisted on the EC's recognition of Croatia and Slovenia; and in the Canadian-Spanish fishing dispute 1995, Britain threatened to veto any EU sanctions taken against Canada.

Although the US actively encouraged European unity during 1948–58, the community system of friendly nation states (most were also NATO members) was an entirely voluntary association of independent states with a Franco-German rapprochement at its core. It continues to provide a permanent forum for diplomacy, tough negotiation and making binding agreements over commerce and trade between themselves and collectively, as the EU, with outsiders (in, for example, GATT and now the World Trade Organization).

Member governments' ministers decide all important matters in the supranational Council of Ministers. They are answerable for their actions to their own national parliaments. Ministers do not report to the European Parliament. There are no members of the EU's executive – the Council of Ministers – in the European Parliament.

Federalism has had nothing to do with European integration to date and the community system of nation states. The temptation to presume and present 45 years of European integration as an inexorable slide towards political federation is to misrepresent what it was actually for and why the ECSC and EEC were really established. It is true that the Commission's role and function has always been to espouse the European Community's interest and now extend the EU's competence through proposals, initiatives and reports that invariably recommend some transfer of national responsibility to supranational control. However, reports like Tindeman's (on EU in 1976) or Marjolin's (on EMU in 1978) were either vetoed, or ignored and shelved by member states at the time. Federalist proposals have also emerged from the EP – such as its February 1984 proposal for a Draft Treaty to establish a European Union. Nevertheless, such themes as EMU and EU continued to have an enduring resonance, reappearing in the Treaty of EU 1992 – the timing of which was largely determined by extraneous events.

For the EP the objective of clawing power from national parliaments towards itself represents a bid for greater functional significance and power, as it is still effectively a huge talking shop where views are expressed that have little political weight behind them. Moreover, it is a parliament kept literally on the move as its sessions and activities are shared between Brussels, Luxembourg and Strasbourg, further reducing its effectiveness as states have never been able to agree on a single home for the EP. Past proposals for reforms from the EP and Commission have not foreshadowed European federation any more than the actions and comments of socialist MPs and groups in Britain's Labour Party reflect the Labour leadership's current agenda and intentions.

A lot of contemporary history is concerned with the pathology of government policy formation and selection. Historians' imperfect hindsight gradually improves with the annual release of new official documents under the 30-year rule, enabling a more accurate picture to emerge through historical detection and discovery.

The eclectic approach adopted here, drawing on research in economic history, political history and international relations, reveals that the portrayal of European integration as some inevitable 'process' leading to federation once underway is untenable. The Pleven Plan, EDC and EPC episode for military and civil integration amounted to a 'tactical diplomatic device for delay' (see Chapter 5) designed to prevent West German rearmament in NATO (which it succeeded in doing for nearly five years). It also protected the political bargaining that underlay the ECSC, so vital for French national economic recovery and security (see Chapter 4).

Since the 1950s European economic integration has only developed and extended its supranational competence (as for example with the SEA 1986) at a pace that actually suited the needs of member states' economies. Integration has not occurred as a result of some intrinsic mechanism or inherent process within the EC system.

Unlike the EDC Treaty of 1952, the 1992 Treaty on EU was ratified and passed into community law; nevertheless, both treaties had two things in common. They were both initially triggered by events outside the community and both were intended to prevent, or at least delay, some political development by Germany, whereas the treaties of Paris 1951, Rome 1957 and SEA 1986 were primarily motivated by the need to construct an appropriate framework to advance Western European states' national economic development.

Even if enough states meet the timetabled technical criteria for monetary union, it remains to be seen whether there is sufficient political will, public support or collective economic need for EMU and consequently the transfer of national monetary policy instruments to a supranational European central bank. Will this represent too great a leap in the dark? Would EMU lead to political federation or confederation? The Paris Treaty 1951 attempted to anticipate and apportion national gains and losses as far as possible in advance to ensure the ECSC's success and safeguard national interests and objectives; the EEC 1958 too contained its 'bargain packages', safeguards, escape clauses and phased introduction of a common market in three stages over a 12-year transition period. Whereas both the economic outcome and political implications of EMU appear far less clear or even wise.

# Bibliography

Adamthwaite, A. (1988) 'The Foreign Office & Policy Making', in J. Young (ed.)
    *The Foreign Policy of Churchill's Peacetime Administration 1951–55*, Leicester:
    Leicester University Press.
Aldcroft, D. (1977) *From Versailles to Wall Street 1919–29*, London: Allen Lane.
Barber, J. and Reed, B. (eds) (1973) *European Community: Vision and Reality*, London:
    Croom Helm.
Beddington-Behrens, E. (1966) *Is There any Choice? Britain Must Join Europe*,
    Harmondsworth: Penguin.
Bell, P. (1986) 'Discussion of European Integration in Britain 1942–45', in W.
    Lipgens (ed.) *Documents on the History of European Integration*, vol. 2, Berlin and New
    York: Walter de Gruyter.
Boyle, P.G. (1982) 'The British Foreign Office and American Foreign Policy, 1947–
    48', *Journal of American Studies*, 16, 3: 373–89.
Council of Europe (1992) *Achievements and Activities*, Council of Europe, Publicity
    and Documentation Service.
Dedman, M. and Fleay, C. (1992) 'Britain and the European Army', *History Today*,
    42, April: 11–14.
Dockrill, S. (1989) 'Britain and the Settlement of the West German Rearmament
    Question in 1954', in M. Dockrill and J.W. Young (eds) *British Foreign Policy
    1945–56*, London: Macmillan.
——(1991) *Britain's Policy for West German Rearmament 1950–55*, Cambridge:
    Cambridge University Press.
Donges, J.B. (1981) 'What is Wrong with the European Communities?', London:
    Institute of Economic Affairs, Occasional Paper 59.
Eden, A. (1960) *Full Circle*, London: Cassell.
Eisenhower, D.D. (1963) *The Whitehouse Years: Mandate for Change 1953–56*.
Fish, S. (1986) 'After Stalin's Death: the Anglo-American Debate over a New Cold
    War', *Diplomatic History*, 10: 333–55.
Foschepoth, J. (1986) 'British Interest in the Division of Germany after the Second
    World War', *Journal of Contemporary History*, 21: 391–411.
Frazier, R. (1984) 'Did Britain Start the Cold War? Bevin and the Truman
    Doctrine', *Historical Journal*, 27, 3: 715–27.
Fursdon, E. (1980) *The European Defence Community: A History*, London: Macmillan.

George, S. (1992) *Politics and Policy in the European Community*, 2nd edn, Oxford: Oxford University Press.

Haas, E.B. (1958) *The Uniting of Europe*, London: Stephens.

HMSO (1971) 'The UK and the European Communities', HMSO cmnd. 4715.

Kindleberger, C.P. (1987) *Marshall Plan Days*, London: Allen & Unwin.

Kirby, S. (1977) 'Britain, NATO and European Security: the Irreducible Commitment', in J. Baylis (ed.) *British Defence in a Changing World*, London: Croom Helm.

Kirkpatrick, I. (1959) *Inner Circle*.

Lipgens, W. (ed.) (1980) *Sources for the History of European Integration 1945–55*, Leyden–London–Boston: Sijthoff.

—— (1982) *A History of European Integration, vol. 1, 1945–47*, Oxford: Clarendon Press.

—— (ed.) (1985) *Documents on the History of European Integration*, vol. 1, Berlin and New York: Walter de Gruyter.

—— (ed.) (1986) *Documents on the History of European Integration*, vol. 2, Berlin and New York: Walter de Gruyter.

Lynch, F. (1984) 'Resolving the Paradox of the Monnet Plan: National and International Planning in French Reconstruction', *Economic History Review*, xxxvii. 2: 229–43.

—— (1993) 'Restoring France: The Road to Integration', in A. Milward, F. Lynch, F. Romero, R. Ranieri and V. Sørensen, *The Frontier of National Sovereignty: History and Theory 1945–92*, London: Routledge.

Mager, O. (1992) 'Anthony Eden and the Framework of Security: Britain's Alternative to the EDC 1951–54', in B. Heuser and R. O'Neill, *Securing Peace in Europe 1945–61*, London: Macmillan.

Mahotière, S. de la (1961) *The Common Market*, London: Hodder.

McDougall, W. (1978) *France's Rhineland Diplomacy 1914–24: The Last Bid for a Balance of Power in Europe*, Princeton: Princeton University Press.

Milward, A.S. (1982) 'The Committee of European Economic Co-operation (CEEC) and the Advent of the Customs Union', in W. Lipgens, *History of European Integration, vol. 1, 1945–47*, Oxford: Clarendon Press.

—— (1984) *The Reconstruction of Western Europe 1945–51*, London: Methuen.

—— (1992) *The European Rescue of the Nation State*, London: Routledge.

Milward, A.S., Lynch, F., Romero, F., Ranieri, R. and Sorensen, V. (1993) *The Frontier of National Sovereignty: History and Theory 1945–92*, London: Routledge.

Newton, C.C.S. (1984) 'The Sterling Crisis of 1947 and the British Response to the Marshall Plan ', *Economic History Review*, xxxvii, 3, August: 391–408.

Pinder, J. (1983) 'History, Politics and Institutions of the EC', in A.M. El-Agraa (ed.) *Britain Within the European Community*, London: Macmillan.

—— (1986) 'Federal Union 1939–41', in W. Lipgens (ed.) *Documents on the History of European Integration*, vol. 2, Berlin and New York: Walter de Gruyter.

—— (1991) *European Community: The Building of a Union*, Oxford: Oxford University Press.

Priebe, H. (1973) 'European Agricultural Policy – a German Viewpoint', in J. Barber and B. Reed (eds) *European Community: Vision and Reality*, London: Croom Helm.

Public Record Office, Foreign Office Papers, FO371, FO800 files.

Reynolds, D. (1980) 'Competitive Co-operation: Anglo-American Relations in World War Two', *Historical Journal*, 23, 1: 233–45.

—— (1988) 'Britain and the New Europe: The Search for Identity since 1940', *Historical Journal*, 31, 1: 223–39.

Romero, F. (1993) 'Migration as an Issue in European Interdependence and Integration: The Case of Italy', in A. Milward, F. Lynch, F. Romero, R. Ranieri and V. Sorensen, *The Frontier of National Sovereignty: History and Theory 1945–92*, London: Routledge.

Schlain, A., Jones, P. and Sainsbury, K. (1977) *British Foreign Secretaries*.

Thatcher, M. (1993) *The Downing Street Years*, London: HarperCollins.

Urwin, D. (1991) *The Community of Europe: A History of European Integration Since 1945*, London: Longmans.

Wallace, W. (1982) 'Europe as a Confederation: The Community and the Nation State', *Journal of Common Market Studies*, xxi, nos. 1 and 2, Sept/Dec: 57–68.

Watt, D.C. (1980) 'Sources for the History of the European Movement', in W. Lipgens (ed.) *Sources for the History of European Integration 1945–55*, Leyden–London–Boston: Sijthoff.

Williams, P. (1954) *Politics in Post-War France*, London: Longmans.

Young, J. (1984) *Britain, France and the Unity of Europe 1945–51*, Leicester: Leicester University Press.

—— (1985) 'Churchill's "No" to Europe: The "Rejection" of European Union by Churchill's Post-War Government, 1951–52', *Historical Journal*, 28, 4: 923–37.

—— (1986) 'Churchill, the Russians and the Western Alliance: The Three Power Conference at Bermuda, December 1953', *English Historical Review*, October.

—— (ed.) (1988) *The Foreign Policy of Churchill's Peacetime Administration 1951–55*, Leicester: Leicester University Press.

—— (1989) 'The Parting of the Ways? Britain, the Messina Conference and the Spaak Committee June–December 1955', Chap. 9, in M. Dockrill and J.W. Young (eds) *British Foreign Policy 1945–56*, London: Macmillan.

# Index

ABC weapons policy 89
Acheson, Dean 41, 44, 45, 60, 76, 79
'Action Committee of all the Non-
  Communist Political Parties and
  Trade Unions of the Six' 99, 102
Adamthwaite, A. 108
Adenauer, Konrad: common market
  policy 98–9, 103–5, 109; EDC
  policy 74–6, 88, 91; election (1949)
  44; Franco-German alliance 2, 63,
  64, 115–16; objectives 91;
  rearmament issue 71–6, 89
Africa 46, 113
Aldcroft, D. 32–3
Algeria 101
Allied Coal and Steel Control Boards
  58
Allied Control Commission 59
Allied-German Contractual
  Agreement 76
Allied High Commission 63
Alsace-Lorraine 57
Amendment Treaty 96
Argentina 117, 131
Asia 46, 71, 84, 113
Association for European Co-
  operation 16
Attlee, Clement 20, 72
Australia 42, 67, 113, 122
Australian–Japanese Trade
  Agreement 113
Austria 12, 110, 128

Baltic States 24
Barber, J. 122

Basic Law 43
Beddington-Behrens, E. 107, 122
Belgium: Communist Party 35;
  currency 46, 51; ECSC 57, 62, 64,
  67, 68, 95; EDC 92; EEC votes 117;
  empire 31, 46; Euratom 98;
  German trade 14, 42; industry 34,
  112; NATO 28; OEEC 50; Ouchy
  Convention 12; US relations 50, 52
Bell, Philip 21
Benelux: Brussels Treaty 39; ECSC 13,
  62; EDC 81, 82, 87; EEC 13, 95, 98,
  115; Ruhr policy 52; steel
  production 59
Berlin 16, 28, 39, 44, 59, 71, 84
Berlin Wall 3, 120
Bermuda 86
Beveridge, Sir William 19, 20, 21, 22
Bevin, Ernest: Council of Europe
  policy 27, 28; Customs Union policy
  37–40; death 108; NATO policy 72,
  76–8; Schuman Plan 65–6; US
  relations 25, 35–7, 39–40; Western
  Union policy 39–40, 48, 107
Beyen, Jacques 98–9, 102
Bidault, Georges 48, 59, 84
Bismarck, Otto von 3
Bizone (Bizonia) 27–8, 49, 52, 54, 60
Bizone Agreement 24
Blum, Leon 27
Boekler, Hans 64
Bohr, Niels 70
Bolsheviks 16
Bonn 66, 75, 76, 87–9, 113

**LEEDS COLLEGE OF BUILDING LIBRARY**
NORTH STREET
LEEDS LS2 7QT
Tel. (0113) 222 6097 and 6098